Praise for *New Poets of Native Nations*

"This twenty-first century of Native poetry is marked by digital singing and storytelling, dislocated relocation, and moments of perception that float like motes in the eyes of Creation. As indigenous peoples, we are always moving and always have been, from Sky to Earth, from East to West, North to South, and back up again. The root of poetry is song-making on lonely dirt roads, or with ears at the apex of sunrise as we listen for something to happen from our singular sound sculptures, for change to happen. That doesn't change no matter the century or in the measure of time that has no description. Here are twenty-one new (and not-so-new) Native poets, writing in English and sometimes our original languages still listening and translating into language what is given to give back. These twenty-one new poets, like their predecessors, are emerging from the Earth or falling from the Sky, from industrial streets, boarding schools, fast cars, all-night tribal or city dances, MFA programs, and bureaucratic lines. Beauty threads with squalor. This is Earth. What a collection Heid E. Erdrich has made of so many original and fresh Native voices, from so many places, gathered here, right here; it is happening, this new Native Nations poetry." —Joy Harjo

"*New Poets of Native Nations* is an astounding collection of writers whose varied works most readers have not yet witnessed. Much of the poetry reveals the confident and unreserved presence of a hybrid language of poetics that does not usually exist inside the boundaries of our earlier concepts of poetry. 'Boundaries' is the key word here, as the writing travels beyond poetic maps of the past. Land and water are contained here, as island and ocean, earth and river, and clouds and grasslands—suddenly and shockingly the grass in the mouth of a trader who had starved the people of food, land, and life. Now, ours is also an environment of new and indecent pesticides, lead-filled waters not revealed to the people drinking it, yellow toxic tainted rivers, all of these new kinds of genocide. As earlier writers held, poetry is a significant method for decolonizing ourselves. Many came together at the momentous event at Standing Rock: such centuries-old struggles to save lands, water, and other elements of our world make the work an intertribal event. A reader of this book finds the genetic and heartfelt circle of history in the cutting edge of each writer's language, which becomes the new old work of hands from the earth bones of indigenous peoples. Such creation and labor revealed in these poems make for a watershed anthology, one of inventive inspiration, of *breath*, a gift to us from the many writers collected here." —Linda Hogan

"At their best, anthologies minimize canonization and maximize community and conversation. In *New Poets of Native Nations*, Heid E. Erdrich invites twenty-one innovative voices to talk to each other and us, and the result is remarkable. I love how this generous collection integrates work from established writers such as Gordon Henry, Jr., LeAnne Howe, and Janet McAdams with newer poets like Natalie Diaz, Jennifer Elise Foerster, Layli Long Soldier, and Tommy Pico, and in so doing illustrates the incredible diversity of contemporary Indigenous poetry. This is an important book not just for Native American writing but for American literature and American history."

—Dean Rader

"It's long past time we had a book like this one, with Native poets of many dispositions securely, as Sy Hoahwah says, 'at the center of the center of the center of things.' They don't—and that's one of the great things about this book—have all that much in common on first read. They don't need to announce their presence or their existence (though they do that too); they can go in all directions, counting on Native and on modernist models, making it old, making it new, stretching and breaking the frames of lyric, explaining and refusing to explain, going on with the exasperated urbanity of Tommy Pico or getting specific about the ice with the wonderful dg nanouk okpik. They stand together not so much in the particular language they choose, as in what they resist: erasure, homogeneity, all the white whatevers that these poets' lines blow away. These poets write in a very contemporary English—sometimes; they also, sometimes, write with and in and for other languages. 'The swamp where / my calling becomes your calling' exists in Margaret Noodin's Anishinaabemowin first, and in a language I can read only afterward, and that's as it should be. Craig Santos Perez casts a net or a word grid broad enough to encompass more concepts than you can fit on any map. Gordon Henry, Jr. declares seriously for the migrants, for the displaced or dispossessed 'among the almost decolonized,' trying hard to imagine 'true sunrise'; Brandy Nālani McDougall finds comic outrage by 'cooking Captain Cook.' Overall, it's a serious counterblast and a congeries of movements and, above all, a large set of poems that can stand on their own, or arrange themselves into formations. Their authors write in compressed lines and in economical versets and prose paragraphs, in terse song forms, in chants, in conversation; they write who they are, they write out of defiance, they write out of loyalty, to and for and about nations, places, collectives, real people, and yet, as Layli Long Soldier has it, 'Everything is in the language we use.' Heid E. Erdrich has done long-awaited and patient and generous work in finding and selecting and collecting these poets from many nations, climates, traditions, and even time zones. *New Poets of Native Nations* is something we need."

—Stephanie Burt

NEW POETS OF NATIVE NATIONS

NEW

POETS OF

NATIVE NATIONS

Edited by Heid E. Erdrich

Graywolf Press

Compilation and introduction copyright © 2018 by Heid E. Erdrich
Permission acknowledgments appear on pages 281–282.

This publication is made possible, in part, by the voters of Minnesota through a Minnesota State Arts Board Operating Support grant, thanks to a legislative appropriation from the arts and cultural heritage fund, and a grant from the Wells Fargo Foundation. Significant support has also been provided by Target, the McKnight Foundation, the Lannan Foundation, the Amazon Literary Partnership, and other generous contributions from foundations, corporations, and individuals. To these organizations and individuals we offer our heartfelt thanks.

Published by Graywolf Press
250 Third Avenue North, Suite 600
Minneapolis, Minnesota 55401

www.graywolfpress.org

Published in the United States of America

ISBN 978-1-55597-809-9

6   8   10   9   7   5

Library of Congress Control Number: 2017953354

Cover design: Mary Austin Speaker
Cover art: Sherwin Bitsui, *Nizhónigó náásgóó naaneeká dó*

CONTENTS

Introduction Twenty-One Poets for the Twenty-First Century ~ xi
  Heid E. Erdrich

Tacey M. Atsitty ~ 3
  Anasazi
  Nightsong
  Downpour
  Paper Water
  Elegy for Yucca Fruit Woman
  Hole through the Rock

Layli Long Soldier ~ 15
  38
  Whereas I Did Not Desire in Childhood
  Whereas Re-solution's an Act
  Obligations 1
  Obligations 2

Tommy Pico ~ 29
  from *IRL*
  from *Nature Poem*
  from *Junk*

Margaret Noodin ~ 45
  Waawiindamojig / The Promisers
  Okanan / Bones
  Winiiam Aagimeke / William Making Snowshoes
  Agoozimakakiig Idiwag / What the Peepers Say
  Jiikimaadizi / A Joyful Life
  Mazinbii'amawaan / Sending Messages

Laura Da' ~ 55
A Mighty Pulverizing Machine
The Haskell Marching Band
Passive Voice
Quarter Strain

Gwen Nell Westerman ~ 65
Owotaŋna Sececa
Linear Process
Genetic Code
Quantum Theory
Dakota Homecoming
Theory Doesn't Live Here
Undivided Interest

Jennifer Elise Foerster ~ 75
Leaving Tulsa
Pottery Lessons I
Birthmark
Chimera
Blood Moon Triptych
Canyon

Natalie Diaz ~ 91
Dome Riddle
Other Small Thundering
American Arithmetic
The First Water Is the Body

Trevino L. Brings Plenty ~ 107
For the Sake of Beauty
The Sound of It
Part Gravel, Part Water, All Indian
Blizzard South Dakota
Northeast Portland
Not Just Anybody Can Have One
Red-ish Brown-ish

Plasmic Kiln
Song Syntax Cycle

dg nanouk okpik ~ 121
Warming
Her/My Arctic Corpse Whale
The Weight of the Arch Distributes the Girth of the Other
A Year Dot
Dog Moon Night at Noatak
She Travels

Julian Talamantez Brolaski ~ 131
Blackwater Stole My Pronoun
In the Cut
What Do They Know of Suffering, Who Eat of Pineapples Yearround
As the Owl Augurs
Stonewall to Standing Rock
Horse Vision
The Bear and the Salmon
When It Rains It Pours
The Bear Was Born

Sy Hoahwah ~ 145
Anchor-Screws of Culture
Toward Mount Scott
Ever Since I Can Remember
What Is Left
Before We Are Eaten
Glitter
Hinterlands
Hillbilly Leviathan

Craig Santos Perez ~ 155
from *Lisiensan Ga'lago*
from *The Legends of Juan Malo* [a Malologue]
Ginen *the Micronesian Kingfisher* [I Sihek]
Ginen *Tidelands* [Latte Stone Park] [Hagåtña, Guåhan]

(First Trimester)
(Papa and Wākea)
(I Tinituhon)

Gordon Henry, Jr. ~ 167
Simple Four Part Directions for Making Indian Lit
How Soon
Dear Sonny:
Among the Almost Decolonized
The Mute Scribe Recalls Some Talking Circle

Brandy Nālani McDougall ~ 181
The Petroglyphs at Olowalu
On Cooking Captain Cook
Pele'aihonua
Papatuanuku
This Island on Which I Love You
Genesis

M. L. Smoker ~ 193
Casualties
Crosscurrent
Equilibrium
We are the ones
Heart Butte, Montana

LeAnne Howe ~ 203
A Duck's Tune
Finders Keepers: Aboriginal Responses to European Colonization
Ballast
Catafalque
Catafalque II
The Rope Seethes

Cedar Sigo ~ 213
Now I'm a Woman
Thrones
Green Rainbow Song

Things to Do in Suquamish
Taken Care Of
Aquarelle
Light Unburied, Unchained
Double Vision

Karenne Wood ~ 227
Amoroleck's Words
My Standard Response
In Memory of Shame
Abracadabra, an Abcedarian
Bartolomé de las Casas, 1542
The Poet I Wish I Was

Eric Gansworth ~ 239
Speaking through Our Nations' Teeth
It Goes Something Like This
Repatriating Ourselves
Snagging the Eye from Curtis
A Half-Life of Cardio-Pulmonary Function
. . . Bee

Janet McAdams ~ 253
The Hands of the Taino
Leaving the Old Gods
Ghazal of Body
from *"The Collectors"*
Tiger on the Shoulder
Hunters, Gatherers
Earthling

Author Notes ~ 269
Editor's Acknowledgments ~ 279
Permissions ~ 281

INTRODUCTION
Twenty-One Poets for the Twenty-First Century

These poems create a place, somewhere we could go. The place of this poetry feels like a familiar country, even though it is made from many nations. This is not to say that poems are lands—certainly not our lands, which we protect rather than open—and yet these poems do create space. Here in these pages, I can show you the brilliantly lit dimension I have visited for several years. Here is poetry of a new time—an era of witness, of coming into voice, an era of change and of political and cultural resurgence—a time shared within this anthology in poetry forceful and subtle, hysterical and lyrical, ironic and earnest, sorrowful and joyful, and presented in ways harder to define, but made of the recent now, the lived realities that poets of Native nations write.

Native nations are our homelands, our political bodies, our heritages, and the places that make us who we are as Natives in the United States of America. More than 566 Native nations exist in the U.S. and yet "Native American poetry" does not really exist. Our poetry might be hundreds of distinct tribal and cultural poetries as well as American poetry. The extraordinary poets gathered in *New Poets of Native Nations* have distinct and close ties to specific indigenous nations—including Alaskan Native and island nations. Most are members or citizens of a tribe: Dakota, Diné, Onondaga, Choctaw, and Anishinaabe/Ojibwe (my tribe), and more than a dozen others. These nations determine their own membership and their own acceptance of descendants. My criterion that a poet have a clear connection to a Native nation has nothing to do with blood quantum, the federal basis for recognition of American Indians. Race also has nothing to do with it. Geography is not a factor. These poets live on reservations, in nations, and in cities or towns. Some of their reservations and homelands are urban; most are rural. Many of these poets have relatives across the borders of Mexico and Canada. Most are multiracial. They are also a diverse group in terms of age, gender, education, and poetic styles, but they have one thing in common. Not one of them identifies as "Native American" alone.

For this book, I gave myself the joyful, challenging, and ultimately uncomfortable task of selecting just twenty-one poets of Native nations from dozens and dozens of fine writers whose first books were published after the year 2000. I chose the year not because it defines a literary movement or even a generation, but because it is a marker after which poets of Native nations began publishing first books in greater numbers than before. Similarly, the "new" in the title does not mean young, but new to book publication in this century. While much of the work in this anthology is new or recent, I also chose previously published poems. My focus is on authors' first books and poems that convey poetic vision and promise. First books are gateways, the launching of careers, and the way these poets influence and teach other poets. Many of these poets won first book awards or book competitions. Several were given publication opportunities through the efforts of poet-editors Joseph Bruchac, Allison Hedge Coke, Geary Hobson, and Janet McAdams. I asked contributors to tell me about their first book experience, and I incorporated their answers into "author notes" along with their suggestions for reading "newer" new poets whose first books are eagerly anticipated. I also asked them about mentors and was surprised to see how often they mentored one another. Solidarity among Native writers, and involvement in professional literary associations, as well as increased access to education and mentorship experiences, particularly through the Institute of American Indian Arts, are no doubt some of the reasons publication has opened up for poets of Native nations in the twenty-first century. Resurgence of culture, the urgency of environmental and social crisis, and the rise of social media are no doubt compelling reasons these authors are publishing as well. Whatever the catalyst, first books are coming out so fast that unfortunately I was unable to include some of the very recent new poets mentioned by several contributors.

While these poets are new to publishing in this century, "new" is not a theme here. In fact, there is no theme to this anthology. However, there are a few commonalities I note: uses of indigenous languages, hybrid styles, and allusions to or direct mentions of other writers from Native nations. Together, while creating work on their own terms, these new poets from dozens of distinct cultures present a vast diversity of literary approaches and national stances. Many of these new writers stretch genre boundaries to include image, song, film, visual art, dance, and history in their performances and presentations of their works as well as publish in multiple literary genres. Many of these new writers advance indigenous language revitalization in their work as translators and teachers, and by incorporating their original languages in their poems in English. Yet, while these generalities about these poets hold true for many, this book does not seek to define a shared aesthetic or cultural context. Instead, *New Poets of Native Nations* collects across a shared experience. These are writers who have grappled with, defined, and redefined the notion of "Native American literature." As their author notes suggest, they have done so through reading and working with other Native writers of the twentieth century (sometimes called the Native American Renaissance) and those poets who closely followed in the late twentieth century. This new poetry stands in relation to generations, but it does not bow to that context.

Native American and American Indian poetry anthologies are old. Critic Dean Rader in 2017 wrote: "That a comprehensive anthology of Indigenous American poetry has not been published since 1988 is utterly depressing." At work on *New Poets of Native Nations*, I knew he was correct both in fact and in feeling. Just a few anthologies of Native American poetry have been published in the past thirty years—none comprehensive of U.S. Native poets alone. Individual collections of writings by members of a specific tribe or region, mixed-genre anthologies, and works focused on women writers have been more regularly, but not frequently, produced. Even the 1988 anthology Rader refers to ends before the beginnings of the careers of late twentieth-century poets of Native nations such as Esther Belin, Kimberly Blaeser, Adrian Louis, Deborah Miranda, Elise Paschen, James Thomas Stevens, Laura Tohe, Luci Tapahonso, Mark Turcotte, and Ofelia Zepeda, to mention just a few. In addition, most Native American poetry anthologies have been published by university presses and are less visible to a general audience. Internet searches for best-selling anthologies under the category of "Native American" or "American Indian" poetry return books published in 1918, 1996, 1988, and 1984, in that order. Clearly, it is time for something new.

The idea for this anthology came to me when I noticed a prominent poet and literary critic's social media post asking for names of contemporary Native American poets. A few good answers were offered eventually. But responses also suggested the names of nineteenth-century tribal orators and worse—the names of known ethnic frauds, of which there are several, and even those who use American Indian–sounding pen names who are white. I looked at all the poetry lovers following the post on social media and it struck me that if an important critic of American poetry asked for general input about Native American poets and got very few names of poets from specific Native nations in response, then we Native Americans writing poetry are dangerously obscure and—worse again—obscured by poets who are not Native to any indigenous nation.

Even as I saw that post asking for names of contemporary Native American poets, I knew the answers were a direct result of what Rader found depressing. Readers are being informed by outdated anthologies. As an editor and judge on panels for literary prizes, I have found among my peer poets and critics a general lack of understanding of what Native American writing looks like, what it might be about, what styles it might choose, and how it can be recognized within the whole of American poetry. It has seemed to me that, unless our poetry conforms to some stereotypical notion of Native American history and culture in the past tense or unless it depicts spiritual relationship to the natural world of animals and plants and landscape, it goes unrecognized. We do and we do not write of treaties, battles, and drums. We do and we do not write about eagles, spirits, and canyons. Native poetry may be those things, but it is not only those things. It is also about grass and apologies, bones and joy, marching bands and genocide, skin and social work, and much more. But who would know?

Although a few poets of Native nations are now producing work within the mainstream of American literary publishing, very little poetry by Natives reaches a large audience—few readers are exposed to multiple indigenous authors at a bookstore or library or even in an academic course. There's simply not enough of our poetry out there where readers can find it. There is no current basis upon which others might understand what poetry by Native Americans is today, in the twenty-first century. Consequently, I have witnessed editors and prize jurors choose poets they *think* are Native American. The result is that more often than you would imagine, what is selected is work by non-Natives. This poetry not only misrepresents the lived realities of Native people, but it does our communities real harm by presenting another's view as our own. Poets who misrepresent themselves as members of Native nations defy each nation's right to determine its own membership. Native American–themed poetry by non-Natives contributes to the erasure we have so long experienced and that has overwritten our identities in ways that confuse young people who are already at risk and struggling to forge an identity. It is often said that we original inhabitants of the Western Hemisphere are the most written about peoples on earth. But our own writing is often ignored or placed in restrictive contexts that keep us in the past and far from the words *contemporary* or *new*. This anthology is meant to bring new audiences to poets of Native nations, including Native audiences, and readers who might then start seeing actual Native-created poetry as part of the larger American poetry conversation.

As I conceived of this book, I wanted to select and present a substantial and strong gathering of work by U.S. Native writers. I wanted to avoid the ways Native American poetry, most edited by non-Natives, has been presented—with a lot of apparatus and within binary notions of an easily digestible "American Indian" history or tradition in order to tie contemporary to past in a kind of literary anthropology. I did not want to add to the body of literature that allows "Indians" to exist in the past, or in relation to the past, but remain invisible in the world we all inhabit now.

I also wanted this book to gather engaging poets in a literary context and within the general market for American poetry. As one who publishes and edits in an American Indian series, I recognize that anthologies from academic presses that do include living Native writers promote those poets, but they also create a kind of isolation. American Indian literary series expressly appeal to those seeking Native American work, so no matter how well-meaning the editors, the work we publish has a very hard time breaking through to a general audience. To put it another way, if you are not looking for authors from Native nations, you rarely find them in the usual places you look for poetry. To put it yet another way, if you are looking at poetry in general, you won't often stumble upon poets of Native nations since literary publishers tend to have only one or two of us per list.

One of the ways into publishing that many of the poets included here have taken is to submit manuscripts for book awards, but after that, the second book can be quite a challenge. My own publishing arc is an example. My first book was published as a prizewinner in an anonymous competition. When I sought publication of my second book, I was told by more than one publisher that it was "too bad we already have our Indian poet." That seems shocking now, but it is still true. I moved on to presses that published several Native writers.

After my first book, I determined to be published with other Native American and Ojibwe/Anishinaabe poets and luckily, those opportunities existed because of the work of Janet McAdams and Gordon Henry, two contributors to this anthology. Their influence can be felt here. More than half of the first books by the poets in *New Poets of Native Nations* are published in series for Native / American Indian and indigenous authors. A few are published by very small literary presses whose distribution is regional, and the very fewest have publishers that regularly publish poetry and that have a national audience and national distribution. Imagine if the same were true of any other culture or racial group in the United States?

The writers in this anthology deserve to be read along with their peers, in the context of the manifold diversity of American poetry, and among the best poets publishing today—especially because some of them are considered the best and most exciting new poets in American literature. Poets in this anthology have won awards from PEN America, the Native Arts and Cultures Foundation, the National Endowment for the Arts, the Lannan Foundation, USA/United States Artists, and other notable organizations. It is my pleasure to present new work by poets whose first books range in age from a few months to nearly eighteen years. Some of these poets have become well known, but to some readers they will be a revelation. I am pleased to introduce all twenty-one poets to a larger audience, perhaps one new to the reality of our persistence as nations. At a time of great change for everyone in this world we all share, it seems people are looking to us, to Indigenous people, perhaps because we have persisted through great change. The time for a new anthology of writings by poets of Native nations is right. Enjoy this place, this space, this dimension these writers open where we can engage deeply with the work of poets whose nations' long tenure in this place tell us something new and enduring at once.

Heid E. Erdrich
July 2017

NEW POETS OF NATIVE NATIONS

TACEY M. ATSITTY

Tacey M. Atsitty, Diné, is Tsénahabiłnii (Sleep Rock People) and born for Ta'neeszahnii (Tangle People) from Cove, Arizona. She is a recipient of the Truman Capote Literary Trust Award in Creative Writing, Corson-Browning Poetry Prize, Morning Star Creative Writing Award, and Philip Freund Prize. She holds bachelor's degrees from Brigham Young University and the Institute of American Indian Arts and an MFA in creative writing from Cornell University.

Atsitty's first book is *Rain Scald* (2018).

Anasazi

How can we die when we're already
prone to leaving the table mid-meal
like Ancient Ones gone to breathe
elsewhere. Salt sits still, but pepper's gone
rolled off in a rush. We've practiced dying
for a long time: when we skip dance or town,
when we chew. We've rounded out
like dining room walls in a canyon, eaten
through by wind—Sorry we rushed off;
the food wasn't ours. Sorry the grease sits
white on our plates, and the jam that didn't set—
use it as syrup to cover every theory of us.

Nightsong

TO THE GORGE DWELLERS

With no fire, you offer
nothing. Say,

a body found, fall creek
gorge. Eventual

it is, meaning to happen.
Meaning to say,

Dear fellow _____,
It is with deep

Name—Name—
Name, strung like

hair. Water strands
made old, made

white. Too close
to dark. Second tragedy

fall creek throat.
Repeated repeated loss.

Thirst-in almanac
of the gorges. Litany

of wrists. Look
down at your wrists,

down here where
the thick laps

the lips. Where you
haven't been taught:

pull yourself out of
the plunge pool

and look for fire, look
for rings shifted

to your thumb and
forefinger. There, like

vapor wrapping you
in strips. In this falling

moment, cities
sink into the depths,

drown. The earth
face carried up and

away in the current of
a whirlwind, where water

and mountains hide
in deep blue. What faces

bring: a reservoir filled,
following the night

when day fell into day,
soon followed by night

into night to night,
thrice with no moon,

thrice with no flame—
kept in the thick thick.

Downpour

I asked him down here:

where virgin belts dangle from my thighs

where my sash belt pulls the sky in, knuckles go white, and all
without a moan

where leaves turn so quickly, already red with winter

where we wait for deluge, but it never comes

not yet ripe, only vocables can embody

Down here, I can't pull out of this tune to utter

the cowardice of hand and tongue   what I wanted

I can't tear myself from this heap of blankets; this rocking comfort, my—

self: the only one I allow

and our son, I leave him, like a monster, cooing in the next gorge over

~

I can't sing over the onrush of falling water, that pounding connect from
mouth to base

lick cloudburst, the way I want

Down here, I speak with a tongue of cedar: bark and kindle

the clouds last night, they held back

But like I said, we shouldn't chant what's not ours

he sacks himself up for me to unravel

a bag of pears. I give one to him, and it gushes with each pull of skin

~

And still I can't tear away from these blankets

even when he says he's ready for downpour:

I offer him my hand to guide me down the gorge

      But don't play my flute for him; I don't want him to fall in—

with me, like I did. I strum him so thinly, and still he chants

      I am left to cramp, my entire body over

           ~

I bring him down here to let my hair loose, then ask him to put it in a knot

      my confidence is worn to warps, a bald fringe

my breath no longer shapes syllables of his name

he says rain and I go beautifully together

      what it means to apologize

how I curl my hair even though my wrists ache for him

how my nails chip before the moons push on through

how I cross my legs for him as he blows at rain

      his fingers wrap our silence

how I prefer the heavens to rainfall

      how for him, I am all of this—as sorry as I am when I say,

      The sky is so hollow from child.

Paper Water

X threads us into rope, a weave of human
arms X-ed down a canyon wall. Voice

writes nights like these and calls
for complete night, without

scraps of light or dissonance or stuttered
cries. Crumble of tree limbs: X, there

we are again. This is how far we climb
for life. We'd rub out before reaching

the ground, where water cuts—
Once a man had only water to pray with.

Once life is the blur of a windmill,
each crisscross sets another arm

to bark. Cessation of the line; break
it up there. Article X: delineate marginal

arcs, say everything within windmill shot—
Whereas injury to water was writ

and concluded: how far inside earth
will they reach? Whereas for groundwater,

they steady their wrists for a slow up-stitch
across their own eyelids.

Elegy for Yucca Fruit Woman

Without me, she said. Go—
I'm going to the rock
that once had wings. My life
rolls like rock clods
down a volcanic throat, circling
the tips of big winds beneath

~

poised arms   *wing bone, surrounded
and closing, dust* hinge. In upstroke, a slow
separate   in landing then takeoff. To take
air, those inward whooshes   as if blessing
oneself: marrow leaving the hollow

~

pop. She knelt with women
filling the earth: mush in tin
after tin, filled in with breaking
sun. Kneeling down, she'd flap
dough with the wood pop,
her hands whirring. The air
bubbles rising with heat ready to—
Later she'd send me to 7-2-11
clenching quarters for—

~

at two points: they say a man flew
with a life-feather, quill in hand,
from the top of Shiprock down
to the people, having slain
monster birds. Plumes

and all their vanes ending
in flight after bird strike

~

"A female eagle swooped east,"
she once told me. "It was like gold
whirring in the blue of my wind-
shield. I was in my truck, driving
and listening to Peyote songs
when it happened. I had never seen
so much dust."

~

When skin slats, layered
like stone then collapses—

a red grows gray. Aspen expands
to the hush

of this cedar-filled room. When
her neck grew heavy she said,

"The music helps me; press play":

Hei hei ya wena hei nei, Hei hei ya wena hei nei;
Hei hei ya wena hei nei, nei; Hei hei ya wena hei nei;
Ya na hei ya na hei o weno hei nei;
Ya na hei ya na hei o weno hwoi na hei nei yo wei.

Hole through the Rock

Nothing but slough before you rode me silver. And smooth,
until I shone. I rode in and didn't even see I was gone: the eye

of my navel, sand folds this way all the time. And rain scours
just the same. You hold all the clay. I fall to granule.

But within my whorl, you are winged: doubled and pure,
like the coupling of pebbles in storm water. These enduring

glances from wind on pane say you can see plainly the part
of me you miss. Our palms meet at the fingertips, forming a W:

double which is only half me to whole us. Where our wrists
brush smooth, clay chips curve into this sand swept hollow:

a roil to the usual clink of bone and arc in stone.

This is not about time; it's the closing
of a single us: a gentle
edging into an ellipse.

LAYLI LONG SOLDIER

Layli Long Soldier is an Oglala Lakota poet, writer, and artist. She is a graduate of the Institute of American Indian Arts, and she holds an MFA from Bard College. Long Soldier is a recipient of a 2015 Lannan Literary Fellowship for Poetry, a 2015 National Artist Fellowship from the Native Arts and Cultures Foundation, a 2016 Whiting Award, the 2018 PEN/ Jean Stein Award, and the 2018 National Book Critics Circle Award for poetry.

WHEREAS (2017) is Long Soldier's first collection of poetry.

38

Here, the sentence will be respected.

I will compose each sentence with care, by minding what the rules of writing dictate.

For example, all sentences will begin with capital letters.

Likewise, the history of the sentence will be honored by ending each one with appropriate punctuation such as a period or question mark, thus bringing the idea to (momentary) completion.

You may like to know, I do not consider this a "creative piece."

I do not regard this as a poem of great imagination or a work of fiction.

Also, historical events will not be dramatized for an "interesting" read.

Therefore, I feel most responsible to the orderly sentence; conveyor of thought.

That said, I will begin.

You may or may not have heard about the Dakota 38.

If this is the first time you've heard of it, you might wonder, "What is the Dakota 38?"

The Dakota 38 refers to thirty-eight Dakota men who were executed by hanging, under orders from President Abraham Lincoln.

To date, this is the largest "legal" mass execution in US history.

The hanging took place on December 26, 1862—the day after Christmas.

This was the *same week* that President Lincoln signed the Emancipation Proclamation.

In the preceding sentence, I italicize "same week" for emphasis.

There was a movie titled *Lincoln* about the presidency of Abraham Lincoln.

The signing of the Emancipation Proclamation was included in the film *Lincoln*; the hanging of the Dakota 38 was not.

In any case, you might be asking, "Why were thirty-eight Dakota men hung?"

As a side note, the past tense of hang is *hung*, but when referring to the capital punishment of hanging, the correct past tense is *hanged*.

So it's possible that you're asking, "Why were thirty-eight Dakota men hanged?"

They were hanged for the Sioux Uprising.

I want to tell you about the Sioux Uprising, but I don't know where to begin.

I may jump around and details will not unfold in chronological order.

Keep in mind, I am not a historian.

So I will recount facts as best as I can, given limited resources and understanding.

Before Minnesota was a state, the Minnesota region, generally speaking, was the traditional homeland for Dakota, Anishinaabeg, and Ho-Chunk people.

During the 1800s, when the US expanded territory, they "purchased" land from the Dakota people as well as the other tribes.

But another way to understand that sort of "purchase" is: Dakota leaders ceded land to the US government in exchange for money or goods, but most importantly, the safety of their people.

Some say that Dakota leaders did not understand the terms they were entering, or they never would have agreed.

Even others call the entire negotiation "trickery."

But to make whatever-it-was official and binding, the US government drew up an initial treaty.

This treaty was later replaced by another (more convenient) treaty, and then another.

I've had difficulty unraveling the terms of these treaties, given the legal speak and congressional language.

As treaties were abrogated (broken) and new treaties were drafted, one after another, the new treaties often referenced old defunct treaties, and it is a muddy, switchback trail to follow.

Although I often feel lost on this trail, I know I am not alone.

However, as best as I can put the facts together, in 1851, Dakota territory was contained to a twelve-mile by one-hundred-fifty-mile long strip along the Minnesota River.

But just seven years later, in 1858, the northern portion was ceded (taken) and the southern portion was (conveniently) allotted, which reduced Dakota land to a stark ten-mile tract.

These amended and broken treaties are often referred to as the Minnesota Treaties.

The word *Minnesota* comes from *mni*, which means water; and *sota*, which means turbid.

Synonyms for turbid include muddy, unclear, cloudy, confused, and smoky.

Everything is in the language we use.

For example, a treaty is, essentially, a contract between two sovereign nations.

The US treaties with the Dakota Nation were legal contracts that promised money.

It could be said, this money was payment for the land the Dakota ceded; for living within assigned boundaries (a reservation); and for relinquishing rights to their vast hunting territory which, in turn, made Dakota people dependent on other means to survive: money.

The previous sentence is circular, akin to so many aspects of history.

As you may have guessed by now, the money promised in the turbid treaties did not make it into the hands of Dakota people.

In addition, local government traders would not offer credit to "Indians" to purchase food or goods.

Without money, store credit, or rights to hunt beyond their ten-mile tract of land, Dakota people began to starve.

The Dakota people were starving.

The Dakota people starved.

In the preceding sentence, the word "starved" does not need italics for emphasis.

One should read "The Dakota people starved" as a straightforward and plainly stated fact.

As a result—and without other options but to continue to starve—Dakota people retaliated.

Dakota warriors organized, struck out, and killed settlers and traders.

This revolt is called the Sioux Uprising.

Eventually, the US Cavalry came to Mnisota to confront the Uprising.

More than one thousand Dakota people were sent to prison.

As already mentioned, thirty-eight Dakota men were subsequently hanged.

After the hanging, those one thousand Dakota prisoners were released.

However, as further consequence, what remained of Dakota territory in Mnisota was dissolved (stolen).

The Dakota people had no land to return to.

This means they were exiled.

Homeless, the Dakota people of Mnisota were relocated (forced) onto reservations in South Dakota and Nebraska.

Now, every year, a group called the Dakota 38 + 2 Riders conduct a memorial horse ride from Lower Brule, South Dakota, to Mankato, Mnisota.

The Memorial Riders travel 325 miles on horseback for eighteen days, sometimes through sub-zero blizzards.

They conclude their journey on December 26, the day of the hanging.

Memorials help focus our memory on particular people or events.

Often, memorials come in the forms of plaques, statues, or gravestones.

The memorial for the Dakota 38 is not an object inscribed with words, but an *act*.

Yet, I started this piece because I was interested in writing about grasses.

So, there is one other event to include, although it's not in chronological order and we must backtrack a little.

When the Dakota people were starving, as you may remember, government traders would not extend store credit to "Indians."

One trader named Andrew Myrick is famous for his refusal to provide credit to Dakota people by saying, "If they are hungry, let them eat grass."

There are variations of Myrick's words, but they are all something to that effect.

When settlers and traders were killed during the Sioux Uprising, one of the first to be executed by the Dakota was Andrew Myrick.

When Myrick's body was found,

                                his mouth was stuffed with grass.

I am inclined to call this act by the Dakota warriors a poem.

There's irony in their poem.

There was no text.

"Real" poems do not "really" require words.

I have italicized the previous sentence to indicate inner dialogue, a revealing moment.

But, on second thought, the words "Let them eat grass" click the gears of the poem into place.

So, we could also say, language and word choice are crucial to the poem's work.

Things are circling back again.

Sometimes, when in a circle, if I wish to exit, I must leap.

And let the body   swing.

From the platform.

                              Out

                                      to the grasses.

Whereas I Did Not Desire in Childhood

WHEREAS I did not desire in childhood to be a part of this but desired most of all to be a part. A piece combined with others to make up a whole. Some but not all of something. In Lakota it's haŋké, a piece or part of anything. Like the creek trickling behind my aunt's house where Uncle built her a bridge to cross from bank to bank, not far from a grassy clearing with three tipis, a place to gather. She holds three-day workshops on traditional arts, young people from Kyle and Potato Creek arrive one by one eager to *participate*. They have the option my auntie says to sleep at home and return in the morning but by and large they'll stay and camp even during South Dakota winters. The comfort of being together. I think of Plains winds snow drifts ice and limbs the exposure and when I slide my arms into a wool coat and put my hand to the door knob, ready to brave the sub-zero dark, someone says be careful out there always consider the snow your friend. Think badly of it, snow will burn you. I walk out remembering that for millennia we have called ourselves Lakota meaning friend or ally. This relationship to the other. Some but not all, still our piece to everything;

Whereas Re-solution's an Act

WHEREAS *re-*

solution's an act

of analyzing and re-

structuring complex

ideas into simpler

ones so I place

a black bracket

on either side of

an [idea] I cordon it

to safety away

from national re-

solution the threat

of re-

ductive

[thinking]:

Whereas Native Peoples are [   ] people with a deep and

abiding [   ] in the [   ], and for millennia Native Peoples

have maintained a powerful [   ] connection to this land,

as evidenced by their [   ] and legends;

●

Whereas the Federal Government condemned the [   ],

[   ], and [   ] of Native Peoples and endeavored to as-

similate them by such policies as the redistribution of land under

the Act of February 8, 1887 (25 U.S.C. 331; 24 Stat. 388, chap-

ter 119) (commonly known as the "General Allotment Act"), and

the forcible removal of Native [   ] from their [   ]

to faraway boarding schools where their Native [   ] and

[   ] were degraded and forbidden;

                              [spiritual]

        [belief]   [Creator]

                              [spiritual]

                    [customs]

                                                  [traditions]

    [beliefs]   [customs]

                              [children]   [families]

                                        [practices]

    [languages]

Obligations 1

When I

was young   grew older

I learned from   I taught   I relied on

my mother   my father   my children   my grandchildren

how   reasons   where   to whom   always

to speak   to speak   to speak   to speak

truthfully   carefully   meaningfully

digging stones   threading grasses

from our chests

Obligations 2

As we

embrace   resist

the future   the present   the past

we work   we struggle   we begin   we fail

to understand   to find   to unbraid   to accept   to question

the grief   the grief   the grief   the grief

we shift   we wield   we bury

into light   as ash

across our faces

TOMMY PICO

Tommy Pico is from the Viejas Indian reservation of the Kumeyaay Nation. He is a recipient of a Queer/Art/Mentors fellowship and a 2013 Lambda Writers Retreat fellowship in poetry. Pico cocurates the reading series Poets With Attitude (PWA) with poet Morgan Parker and cohosts the podcast Food 4 Thot.

IRL (2016) is Tommy Pico's first book of poems. *Nature Poem* (2017) is his second collection. Pico's third book is *Junk* (2018).

from *IRL*

Is this ad relevant to you?
We would like to enhance
your ad watching ex-
perience. Yr a garbage
person if you can't
take a good photo,
is the underlying mess-
age of "gay" "culture"
in Brooklyn The concept
of fame in the United
States I hate
having my picture taken,
I say to this photog-
rapher at this party
bc every damn party
has to b photographed
otherwise it doesn't happen
And bc the parties
are so boring, if ppl
weren't posing
there would b nothing
to do but drink. It's
too loud for convos
n they don't let you dance
in the city. He says *oh
come on.* I say calmly
No. n he asks *is this
an Indian thing? Like
does a pic steal yr soul
or something?*

I want to crumple
him up in the palm
of my hand But I
guess it is a NDN

thing in the sense that
I'm NDN n doing
this thing. Posin for pics
is like not being able
to stare into the sun
for too long but kind of the
opposite—blank black lens
crystallizes the uncertainty
within.
Is this good, or bad
is a sentence in a fight
n I hate confrontation.
Why do I have to take
sides? Switzerland has
the strictest privacy laws
on the planet, and I
have the flyest tank
tops in America. Some-
how I feel good about it.
In Kumeyaay
there's a concept for in-
between. Not knowing
how to smile, how you look
bent over a book Waking
up on either coast
feels the exact same
Sometimes you wake up
not knowing how old
you are n if Johnny
is down the hall in
a robe makin eggs. Future
leaders are *wooshed* away
from the tribe in a sort of
boreal way to feel
the greater world, stone

hills etc (this is back
in the day).
This in-between
is like gangbusters
for Muse. It's like cat-
nip to Muse It's throb
of light in-between
the 2 of us Just the 2
of us, you n I. I rub Muse
my neck I'm clenching
my jaw for like 20 mins
waiting for this damn
photog to take damn
pic. In-between
Kumeyaay and Brooklyn—
that it has a word,
even if the word is lost
even if the word doesn't exist
even if I'm lyin to you,
is breath tethering Opens throb
of light inside me. I
don't have the option
of keeping my God
alive by keeping her name
secret b/c the word for her
is gone Keeping secrets
is not possible So I give
everything away I'm out
here all alone trying to wad
up enough obsessions
to replace her and with
it, my God I never got to
know her But strangely
sometimes when I'm cry-
laughing at that scene

in Steel Magnolias or
I can't sing the part in
that Beyoncé song at
karaoke where the music
gets all soft and I try
to croon *ooh baby, kiss me*—
Maud has to take
the mic bc the feeling gets
bigger than my voice n
the feeling I think it's her My God
's shadow walking down a hall-
way away but like I said I lost
my voice n don't know
her name Maybe it's
Wa'ashi or Pemu,
says this clairaudient
to me apropos of nothing
But I'lI never know 4
sure So I can't call after her
n then I'm like, crying
at a Beyoncé song
r u kidding me Teebs get
it together bitch My dad grows
his hair long Black waves
cascade down his back b/c knives
crop the ceremony of his
mother's hair at the NDN boarding
school I cut mine in mourning
for the old life but I grow
my poems long. A dark
reminder on white pages.
A new ceremony. I grab
the mic back from
Maud Flip for a new song to
flash across the karaoke

screen Fist breath low
n ready James
is finally following me
back on Insta so I take a
somewhat *risque*
selfie send it DM
n right after message
OOOPS! omg I
meant to send that
to someone else gosh
so embarrassed oops!
He responds w/
a pic of his computer
screen His phone #
on it so we
text n he's like
come over n I'm like
do u have A/C he says
Yes n I just straight up
drop the mic
n Leave.

from *Nature Poem*

I can't write a nature poem
bc it's fodder for the noble savage
narrative. I wd slap a tree across the face,
I say to my audience.

Let's say I'm at a pizza parlor
Let's say I'm having a slice at the bar this man walks in to pick up his
to-go order
Let's say his order isn't ready yet and he's chatty
Let's say I'm in Portland bc ppl don't tawlk to me in NYC
Let's say he's like, *meatballs are for the baby, pizza's for the little man
Caesar salad's for the wife and the beer* he points to the beer and then
thumbs at himself, *the beer's for me.*

He has one of those cracked skin summer smiles

He keeps talking like I want to hear him
Like he's so comfortable
Like everybody owes him attention

I'm a weirdo NDN faggot

He puts his hands on the ribs of my chair asks do I want to go into the
bathroom with him

Let's say it doesn't turn me on at all

Let's say I literally hate all men bc literally men are animals—

This is a kind of nature I would write a poem about.

We are the last animal to arrive in the kingdom—even science will tell you that.

My father takes me into the hills we cut sage. He tells me to *thank the plant for its sacrifice, son.* Every time I free a switch of it a burst of prayer for every leaf.

I'm swoll on knowing this? Sharing the pride of plants

My mother waves at oak trees. A doctor delivers her diagnosis.

When she ascends the mountains to pick acorn, my mother motherfucking waves at oak trees. Watching her stand there, her hands behind her back, rocking, grinning into the face of the bark—

They are talking to each other.

I am nothing like that, I say to my audience.

I say, *I went to Sarah Lawrence College*

I make quinoa n shit

Once on campus I see a York Peppermint Pattie wrapper on the ground, pick it up, and throw it away. *Yr such a good Indian* says some dick walking to class. So,

I no longer pick up trash.

I can't write a nature poem bc that conversation happens in the Hall of
South American Peoples in the American Museum of Natural History

btwn two white ladies in buttery shawls as they pass a display case of
"traditional" garb from one tribe or another it doesn't really matter to
  anyone

and that word *Natural* in *Natural History* hangs
also *History*
also *Peoples*
hangs as in frames

it's horrible how their culture was destroyed

as if in some reckless storm

but thank god we were able to save some of these artifacts—history is so
important. Will you look at this metalwork? I could cry—

Look, I'm sure you really do just want to wear those dream catcher
earrings. They're beautiful. I'm sure you don't mean any harm, I'm sure
you don't really think abt us at all. I'm sure you don't understand the
concept of off-limits. But what if by not wearing a headdress in yr music
video or changing yr damn mascot and perhaps adding .05% of personal
annoyance to your life for the twenty minutes it lasts, the 103 young ppl
who tried to kill themselves on the Pine Ridge Indian reservation over
the past four months wanted to live 50% more

I don't want to be seen, generally, I'm a natural introvert, n I def don't
want to be seen by white ladies in buttery shawls,
but I will literally die if I don't scream

You can't be an NDN person in today's world

and write a nature poem. I swore to myself I would never write a nature poem. Let's be clear, I hate nature—hate its *guts*

I say to my audience. There is something smaller I say to myself:

I don't hate nature at all. Places have thoughts—hills have backs that love being stroked by our eyes. The river gobbles down its tract as a metaphor but also abt its day. The bluffs purr when we put down blankets at the downturn of the sun and laugh at a couple on a obvi OkCupid date

and even more stellar, the jellybean moon sugars at me. She flies and beams and I breathe.

Fuck that. I recant. I slap myself.

Let's say I live in NYC. Let's say I was the first person in my family to graduate college. Let's say UGH I like watching *New Girl* on Hulu.

This is the difference:

Some see objects in the Earth, where I see lungs. Sky mother falls thru a hole, lands on a turtle.

Hole is my favorite band.

from *Junk*

Picture it: Sicily, 1923 Whoops I mean Thanksgiving dinner w/
family in town from the rez at a midtown resto, blackberries

in the whipped cream while the Washington Redskins blaze on
TV behind us Or last month when police clashed with water

protectors Tore down encampments and elders and children
On the same day milk-toned Oregonian militiamen r acquitted

after armed occupation of land On the same day the Cleveland
Indians r in the World Series during American Indian heritage

month Before, in the past, this world discovered war Berlin
Afghanistan Terracotta Slob War War War in the front of every

newspaper In the back of every noggin Sludgy nympho gummy
bear humps the Haribo package—Body monuments and light

cigarettes Diet Cherry Dr. Pepper and a bag of Hot Cheetos
Cholera epidemic in Haiti where there is no immunity because

Cholera was like the only thing that never befell Hispaniola
Rasp is sassy but Junk is punk Static in its intention Static in

its emotional release Static in the city Buzz of disbelief White-
house domes every convo *We are a part of the rhythm nation* I

get this teaching gig and being an authority figure, let me tell u
is such an emperor has no clothes situation Like being onstage

Very, "I'm more afraid of you than you are of me" Sharon Jones
glides on about being an injured prison guard on Rikers Island

Terry Gross asks, "How were you able to convince the prisoners
that you were strong enough and focused enough to do the job

and keep them in line?" Sharon says "It's the look in my eyes . . .
You could not show fear, and that's one thing I didn't show" Try

it on Saying "pilfer is a fun word" enough times makes it true,
like petticoat coffee cakes and the invention of blue raspberry

Dummy stay on message I never intended to be a professional
NDN but this time of year every1 wants to know do I celebrate

Thanksgiving? Janet is still with us, despite the retreat of
common sense, the retreat of fall, the retreat of Sharon Jones

and David Bowie and Prince and Vanity and Leonard Cohen
Phife Dawg and George Michael Do you remember what it was

like to feel warmth from the sun? It's odd, right? For light to
only be light and not also heat The sun conceals things too, in

its glare It makes sense that it took me the whole year before I cd
entertain talking to u again Back in our crystalline season I was

right 2 suspect worth in yr grace You aren't evil for not loving me
Maybe it's a retrograde situation Look into the sky, yearning to be

someplace else When you gobble gobble so fast it's like dinner
never happened & even now conjuring you feels like a diversion

but yr the reason I started writing this in the first place Michelle
Tea says when you write about someone, you have to be able to

look them in the face Your faces are many Your shoulders are
different colors Sometimes yr EXTREMELY tall and sometimes only

very tall Sometimes yr face is golden smooth and cut like a English
garden Sometimes yr face is lunar, bright chalk white n cratered

Sometimes we were together for six weeks Sometimes eight
months Sometimes I don't know yet We sit still in our gurgle sacks

waiting for each other to change Waiting for our stomachs to glow
pink again in the gallery night But we dimmed Each time we dim

we dimmed differently but we dimmed we did The Metro Link
Light Rail SEPTA MTBA Amtrak Bolt Bus Megabus the Peter Pan

the MAX Metro North Marc Train Charm City Circulator The
opposite of escape A firming in the firmament The couch An

airbed Yoga mat and sometimes just the floor Man punches
woman at bar Man screams at woman in diner Man yells at

woman in a hijab in Queens "Man, man, menace" is like a weird
game of "duck, duck, goose" The hollow taste on the inside of yr

mouth when u haven't eaten all day Make out with boys named
Patrick n Gerald n Martin n David and suck on his finger at the bar

with the empty blue fish tank and random lotto ball cage Drink
Shiners in his backyard Threesomes are awkward af mostly bc

everyone is wasted so it feels like heavy turbulence on the twin
bed in this liver I mean sliver of apartment Last Resort Lagunitas

Goose Island The shot special Two more packages of Reece's Old
Fashioned Narragansett and Jameson on the rocks Whatever

insulates you from the calving face of this gd world When has
sympathy for the oppressor ever worked for us? The poem and

reading the poem become each other Echolocation The sound of
a shape The news leaps through me like a talking dog—unreal,

no? I don't know where the feeling is or what to do with it n
spent most of the day w/ my eyes squeezed shut but then I

went for a run to force feed myself some endorphins Wrote a
few couplets and texted all my friends and went to the rally

and marched bc it felt restorative to blast night with my voice
box and stomp the sidewalks and the streets with friends for

twenty blocks in all directions Whole blocks of avenues in all
directions swell w/peeps shouting MUSLIM RIGHTS ARE

HUMAN RIGHTS and MY BODY MY CHOICE and BLACK LIVES
MATTER and WATER IS LIFE and TRANS LIVES MATTER Then we

got a drink and for a couple hours it seemed like we'd just been
in some horrible dream As if the fog lifted and we could hear

through the static Feel the sun again But it's only growing colder
This is just the beginning And yeah maybe the path back from

complacency is lion's mane but I was afraid a long time b4 these days

MARGARET NOODIN

Margaret Noodin is a descendant of the Grand Portage Band of Lake Superior Chippewa who was raised in Minnesota. Noodin is the author of *Bawaajimo: A Dialect of Dreams in Anishinaabe Language and Literature*. Her poetry is bilingual, produced in Anishinaabemowin and English. She teaches Anishinaabemowin at the University of Wisconsin–Milwaukee, where she is a professor in the English and American Studies departments.

Weweni (2015) is Noodin's first book of poems.

Waawiindamojig / *The Promisers*

Nangodinong	Sometimes
niizhing gimewon	the rain came twice
mii wi apii gii giiwanimowaad.	and that is when they lied.
Akiwenziiyag biiminaanaawaan	The old men twisted
bingwi-waawiindamaadiwinan	the dusty promises
gii waawiindamaadiwaad enji-zaagiding.	they once made as young lovers.
Mindimooyensag gibozaanaawaan	The old ladies baked
dibajimowinan biinish ombishkaa	the tales until they rose
awaasa debwetaagwag.	beyond believability.
Nooshensag ozaagiaawaan	The grandchildren adored them
onzaam gashkitoowaad	for this ability to
anishaa'endamowaad ezhi-maadiziwaad.	re-imagine their lives.
Oniijaanishag gii zegiziwag	Their own children were frightened
onzaam gikendamowaad ingoding	by the idea of what they
waa ezhi-dibaajimowaad.	would say themselves one day.

Okanan / Bones

Apii jiibay bi dagooshin

okanan onandawaabandaanan

gii gaadooyaan baatiindoon

ishkweya'ii ndodengwekaajigan.

Nisimdana-ashi-niswi beshabiiaag

manidoominensag inaabiiginaag

oningwiiganan gaawiin tesiinon

onzowan gaawiin tesiinon.

Niizhtana-ashi-niizhwaaswi nindayaanan

wii aabjitooyaan ji-ezhininjiishiyaan

maagizha giiwitaajiishinidiying
    ji-maamwizhibiiamaang

dibaajimowinan e-waamjigaadeg.

Miidash dibishkoo makwa

ningwayakogaabow

gichikaanan biiskamowaad

mashkawiziwinan ji-maajaayaan.

Okanensan agaasin apii enewewin

When the ghost visits

looking for bones

I have some hidden

behind my mask.

I have a line of thirty-three

beads strung between

an absence of wings

to where there is no tail.

I have twenty-seven of them

I use to make one handprint

or curl together
    to write

stories that can be seen.

And when like a bear

I balance my height

the largest bones wear

ropes of strength in motion.

But the bones smaller than
    sound

gibaakogaadeg nipigemagong ani | are kept in a cage near my
| heart

ziitaaganimiskwimamaangaashkaamagag | where red saltwater waves

bimiwidoowaad kaakazhewaabik | carry calcium
   waabanong mii ningaabii'anong. | east then west.

Gaawiin tesiinon okanan | There are no bones

ninendamowining epichii bwaajigeyaan, | in my mind when I dream,

indooning apii jiim'inan, | on my mouth when I kiss,

nineseng apii mamigaadeg. | on my breath when it is
| taken away.

Gaawiin tesiinon okanan | There are no bones

apii oshkibimaadiziwinkeyaang, | when we make new life,

debiziyaang apii zaagidiyaang, | fall in love satisfied,

mawiyaang, anamaegaazoyaang. | cry or pretend to pray.

Mii sa ongow niibina gego | These are the things

gashkigaadooyaan | I can hide

apii jiibay bi dagooshinod | when the ghost visits

okanan nandawaabandang. | looking for bones.

Winiiam Aagimeke / William Making Snowshoes

Ge-maajimamaangadepon	As frozen flakes fell in clusters
giizis ishpaagoozid, ishpaagonagaag agwajiing	sun high in the sky, snow deep outside
mii dash inaaginang ezhi-inendang	he began to bend his thoughts
naagadawendang debwemigag	considering what is true
gaye gaawiin debwesiinog	and what is not
Skadi'an gaye Bakewizian naagadawenimaad	considering Skadi and Pukwiss
ezhi-giibabaamaagimenid.	and the way they walked on the snow.
Chiwenipanad onji-gii aagimiked	Because it was simplest, he made snowshoes
miigwechwi'aad aagimakoon	thanked the white ash
waazhaabiid miidash waaginaang,	cut the laces and bent the wood,
aazheyaajimowinan gashka'oodeg	all the back stories tangling
gaa nisidotamang inkamigag	what we understand happened
gete-aadizookaanag gashka'oozowaad	all the teaching tales tangling
ezhi-gizhemanidoo naago'idizod.	the way the Creator is revealed.
Apii gii giizhiitaad anokiid gaye bengoziwaad	When his work was done and they were dry
giizikaang makazinan mii biizikawaad agimag	he took off his moccasins, put on the snowshoes

mii bineshiinhgaazod
    ji-babaamikawed
	going out to leave tracks light
	    as a bird

jiimaanbii'ang bagakaagonagaa	writing canoe shapes in the bright snow
epiichi baazhida'ang ziibiwan	as he walked over rivers
jiimaanbii'aad maazikaamikwe	writing kiss shapes on the earth
gaye ode'eng zhawenimaad.	and in the center of the blessed.

Agoozimakakiig Idiwag / What the Peepers Say

Ishkwaa biboon bii'omigag

gaawiin geyabi aabita-

nibwaakaamashkawajisiiwaad

biibaagiyaang ani biibaagiyang.

After the winter waiting

no longer half-

frozen by design

our calling becomes all calling.

Naami-zaasiji-wanagek

agoozimakakiig gii ningizyang

mii zaagidoodeyang mashkiigong

biibaagiyaan ani biibaagiyan.

Under the rippling bark

peepers have thawed

to crawl into the swamp where

my calling becomes your calling.

Dibishkoo didibaashkaa

zhaabwibiisaa zoogipog

ziigwang ziibiskaaj miidash

biibaagiyan ani biibaagiyaan.

a seismic seiche

a synaptic snowstorm

of springtime repetition and

your calling becomes my calling.

Epichii maadaa'ogoyang basweweyang

beshoganawaabmigag aawiyang

waasaganawaabmigag aawiyang

biibaagiyang ani biibaagidiyaang.

As we drift away on our echoes

we are the details

we are the distance and

all calling becomes our calling.

Jiikimaadizi / A Joyful Life

Apii Manidoo-giizisoons basangwaabi — When the sky's eye blinks in December

gaye gaawiin bazhiba'ansiimaan — and I can't spear one of the

ge-bimaadagendamaan dwaa'ibaaning — thoughts swimming past the ice hole

mii mikwendamaan Ode'imini-giizis — I think of the strawberry-moon light

miskwiiwid miskwaa'aasiged giizhigong. — bleeding across a long summer day.

Dagwaagin apii waaboozoog zaagi'agwaa — When I fall in love with autumn rabbits

idash gaawiin debibidasiiwagwaa — but can't hold them close enough

napaaj-aanzo'adoweyang — and all our fur is the wrong color

waawaashkeshikwe mikwenimag — I think of deer woman

ziikipidang ziibiwan ji-gidagaakoonsked. — drinking rivers to make spotted fawns.

Wenpanad gwayakowendamang, — It's easy to change our minds

zhaabwaabiyang, bakobiiseyang — to look through a window, fall into a lake

zanagad gwenibiiyang, — it's harder to quit,

akawaabiyang, bakegaabawiyang — to wait or step off the main path

ji-mikamang ezhi-jiikimaadiziyang. — to discover a joyful life.

Mazinbii'amawaan / Sending Messages

Ningikendaan akiin bakaanadoon | I know there are different worlds

zaam gaa nindaanikoobijiganaanig mazinbii'amawaan | because our ancestors sent them messages

zaam wiijiwag wanishinwaad daawaad noongom | because lost lovers now live in them

zaam gii izhi'iyan zhigo. | because you just said that right now.

Giishkaanaabikaa ina gid'aaw | Are you the carved shoreline

gaye gichigami aawiyaan | and I the sweetwater sea

gemaa washkiyaanimaazoyaan | or am I the shifting wind

gaawiin gikenimisiiyan? | you cannot perceive?

LAURA DA'

Laura Da' is an enrolled member of the Eastern Shawnee Tribe
of Oklahoma. She received a 2015 Native Arts and Cultures
Foundation Fellowship, was a 2015 Jack Straw Writer, and was
a 2014–15 Made at Hugo House fellow. She studied creative
writing at the University of Washington and the Institute of
American Indian Arts. Laura Da' is a public school teacher.

Tributaries (2015) is Da's first full length poetry collection.
It won the American Book Award in 2016. Her chapbook *The
Tecumseh Motel* is published in *Effigies II: An Anthology of New
Indigenous Writing, Pacific Rim* (2014). Her second book is
Instruments of the True Measure (2018).

A Mighty Pulverizing Machine

To each orphaned child—so long as you remain close enough to walk to your living kin you will dance, feast, feel community in food. This cannot stand. Eighty acres allotted.

To each head of household—so long as you remember your tribal words for village you will recollect that the grasses still grow and the rivers still flow. So long as you teach your children these words they will remember as well. This we cannot allow. One hundred and sixty acres allotted.

To each elder unable to till or hunt—so long as your old and injurious habits sing out over the drum or flicker near the fire you cripple our reward. We seek to hasten your end. Eighty acres allotted.

To each widowed wife—so long as you can make your mark, your land may be leased. A blessing on your mark when you sign it and walk closer to your favored white sister. Eighty acres allotted.

To each full blood—so long as you have an open hand, we shall fill it with a broken ploughshare. One hundred and sixty acres allotted.

To each half blood, each quarter strain—so long as you yearn for the broken ploughshare, you will be provided a spade honed to razor in its place. When every acre of your allotment has been leased or sold, you will turn it on yourself. From that date begins our real and permanent progress.

The Haskell Marching Band

In the basement of Haskell Indian School,
she was one of the girls standing assembly style
pressing flour into pie tins.

Long hours at the school's foundry made him crepuscular.
Accustomed to seeing his shadow in waxy pre-dawn light,
he would pause near the basement bakery's vent,
warmth blossoming around his ankles as he placed his boots in the slush
and stomped out a tune that she'd recognize
from the last night's band rehearsal.

After graduation, they married:
the band had to find
another trumpeter—
the quartet a new flutist.

Thirteen summers of work release—
eighteen-hour days and humid hayloft nights
allowed him to buy his trumpet from the music instructor.
The flute stayed behind.

Passive Voice

I use a trick to teach students
how to avoid passive voice.

Circle the verbs.
Imagine inserting "by zombies"
after each one.

Have the words been claimed
by the flesh-hungry undead?
If so, passive voice.

I wonder if these
sixth graders will recollect,
on summer vacation,
as they stretch their legs
on the way home
from Yellowstone or Yosemite
and the byway's historical marker
beckons them to the
site of an Indian village—

Where *trouble was brewing*.
Where, *after further hostilities, the army was directed to enter*.
Where *the village was razed after the skirmish occurred*.
Where *most were women and children*.

Riveted bramble of passive verbs
etched in wood—
stripped hands
breaking up from the dry ground
to pinch the meat
of their young red tongues.

Quarter Strain

I.

First quarter
strain is the hardest.

One hour
September's lecture
on the newest set
of comprehensive learning standards

    sends me roving.

Glasses frame windows,
windows frame listing cedars.

Ozymandias in broadside hangs
by one staple
next to the definition of the doggerel:

    They went to sea in a sieve, they did,
    In a sieve they went to sea.

Shards of eraser—
steampunk spiders
prickly with embedded staples
cling to the ceiling panels.

Rust-font tributaries
dance in the margin
of the galley-print textbook.

My eyes drop
like cannon balls in a mutiny.

Frank red bursts
groping for my spine,
shrill vermillion shrieks.

Little red mouths
    start chanting inside me.

2.

Afternoons dope me.

Sprawled on the floor,
        I wake covered and corralled
by cratered Lego fortresses,
sniffable markers plugged end-to-end,
matchbox cars and fire trucks
in the chaotic parking patterns
        of emergency.

My son is prodding me
to greet him. Say hello.

Say it in Spanish.

Say it again in Tewa. Say it

        in Shawnee.

3.

The surgeon
writes my next act
with a lilac felt-tipped pen
so that as I am unconscious
      she perforates
        her own name first.

Then my abdomen
in four careful slits.

Failed anesthesia,
panicked by the breathing tube,
thrashing on the table
bile and blood aspirate
and rot in my lungs.

In post-operative pneumonia
I return to work

One day teaching
the myth of Phaethon,
Icarus and Daedalus,
Coyote and the Stars,
the story of a trickster
who lifts a whale
      from the lapping waves.

4.

I agonized for years
over my quartered self
but the body
breaks whole.

Even so I end
the year in thrall
to that trickster
of symmetry—
in the propitious
three out of four
survivors.

The deepest wound
bleeds steadily
around the surgical tube;
a long stemmed dahlia
blooming at my side
through all four seasons.

GWEN NELL WESTERMAN

Gwen Nell Westerman is an enrolled member of the Sisseton Wahpeton Dakota Oyate and a citizen of the Cherokee Nation of Oklahoma. Westerman is the author of *Follow the Blackbirds*, poetry in English and Dakota. She is also an award-winning textile artist. Westerman is professor of English and director of the Humanities Program at Minnesota State University, Mankato. She directs the Native American Literature Symposium.

Follow the Blackbirds (2013) is Westerman's first poetry collection. New work includes *Dakota in Minnesota* (2017), and a new poetry volume, *War Mothers Song* (2019).

Owotaŋna Sececa

Hekta ehaŋna
   ḳaŋpi hena
     taku owas
       ecipaś
     hdi ce e
   eyapi.
Tka tokiya taŋhaŋ
   uŋhipi he.
      Toked kiya
       uŋyapi kta he.

        Ina ate kuŋśi uŋkaŋna
        wicayutakupida śni.
        Ikce wicaśtapi śni waŋna
        caże wicoie wocckiya
        kcihdaya nażiŋpi
        wotapi kte heyake toktokca
        wicapażo wicayuhapi.
        Hetaŋhaŋ uŋkicaġapi
        tka tiwahe taku sdodyapi śni.
        Sdodyapi śni.
        Tka waŋna ake ecipaś
       kiya uŋkupi
      ecineś
     hekta ehaŋna
    eyapi taku
   owas ecipaś
  hdi
 ce e.

Linear Process

Our elders say
        the universe is a
            circle.
                    Everything
                returns to its
        beginnings.
But where do we go
        from here?
            Where are
                    our beginnings?

                    Our parents were stripped
                    of their parents
                    names tongues   prayers,
                    lined up for their meals
                    clothes   classes tests.
                    When it was our turn
                    to come into this world,
                    they did not know
                    what family meant
                    anymore.
                    They did not
                    know.
                    Yet even
                from here,
            we can
        see that the
        straightest line
        on a map
    is a
    circle.

Genetic Code

On the edge of a dream,
the songs came.
Condensed from the fog,
like dewdrops on cattails,
they formed perfectly clear.
Whispering through leaves,
heavy voices rise up,
drift beyond night
toward the silent dawn,
and sing.

>*Hekta ehaŋna ded uŋṭipi.*
>*Heuŋ he ohiŋni uŋkiksuyapi kte.*
>*Aŋpetu dena ded uŋṭipi.*
>*Heca ohiŋni uŋdowaŋpi kte.*

Always on still morning air,
they come,
connected by
memories and
song.

Quantum Theory

Cut by a paper razor, I watch blood fill

    a perfectly straight wound on my finger,

Denying the swirl of generations before me and

    the possibility of those held in my dreams.

Illusory, the narrow and unyielding course fills

    in red, then overflows into a galaxy where

Blood carries stories of our origins from

    beyond the stars.

Dakota Homecoming

We are so honored that
      you are here, they said.
We know that this is
      your homeland, they said.
The admission price
      is five dollars, they said.
Here is your button
      for the event, they said.
It means so much to us that
      you are here, they said.
We want to write
      an apology letter, they said.
Tell us what to say.

Theory Doesn't Live Here

My grandparents never talked
about theory, decolonization, or
post-colonial this or that.
They talked about
good times and bad times.
Their self-determination was
not a struggle against
colonialism affecting their
self-imagination.
They worked hard to survive.
They didn't imagine themselves
through story.
They knew themselves
through the stories they heard
as they sat under the kitchen table
listening to the old people talk.
They didn't need theory
to explain where they came from—
they lived it.

Undivided Interest

This is what is left of my land:
>Meridian 05 Township 151N
>Range 064W Section 09
>Acres 40 Type 253500 PA
>IA 708

Letters and numbers.
Fractions.
Undivided interest—divided
among 336 heirs.
My interest equals 0.119 acres.
My ancestor an Indian Account.

Her name was not IA 708.
She was called Tiyowaštewin
and her interest was
undivided.

JENNIFER ELISE FOERSTER

Jennifer Elise Foerster, a member of the Muscogee (Creek) Nation of Oklahoma, is an alumna of the Institute of American Indian Arts, the Vermont College of Fine Arts, and is completing a PhD at the University of Denver. She is the recipient of a 2017 NEA Creative Writing Fellowship and was a Wallace Stegner Fellow.

Foerster is the author of *Leaving Tulsa* (2013) and *Bright Raft in the Afterweather* (2018).

Leaving Tulsa

FOR COSETTA

Once there were coyotes, cardinals
in the cedar. You could cure amnesia
with the trees of our back-forty. Once
I drowned in a monsoon of frogs—
Grandma said it was a good thing, a promise
for a good crop. Grandma's perfect tomatoes.
Squash. She taught us to shuck corn, laughing,
never spoke about her childhood
or the faces in gingerbread tins
stacked in the closet.

She was covered in a quilt, the Creek way.
But I don't know this kind of burial:
vanishing toads, thinning pecan groves,
peach trees choked by palms.
New neighbors tossing clipped grass
over our fence line, griping to the city
of our overgrown fields.

Grandma fell in love with a truck driver,
grew watermelons by the pond
on our Indian allotment,
took us fishing for dragonflies.
When the bulldozers came
with their documents from the city
and a truckload of pipelines,
her shotgun was already loaded.

Under the bent chestnut, the well
where Cosetta's husband
hid his whiskey—buried beneath roots

her bundle of beads. *They tell
the story of our family.* Cosetta's land
flattened to a parking lot.

Grandma potted a cedar sapling
I could take on the road for luck.
She used the bark for heart lesions
doctors couldn't explain.
To her they were maps, traces of home,
the Milky Way, where she's going, she said.

After the funeral
I stowed her jewelry in the ground,
promised to return when the rivers rose.

On the grassy plain behind the house
one buffalo remains.

Along the highway's gravel pits
sunflowers stand in dense rows.
Telephone poles crook into the layered sky.
A crow's beak broken by a windmill's blade.
It is then I understand my grandmother:
When they see open land
they only know to take it.

I understand how to walk among hay bales
looking for turtle shells.
How to sing over the groan of the county road
widening to four lanes.
I understand how to keep from looking up:
small planes trail overhead
as I kneel in the Johnson grass
combing away footprints.

Up here, parallel to the median
with a vista of mesas' weavings,
the sky a belt of blue and white beadwork,
I see our hundred and sixty acres
stamped on God's forsaken country,

a roof blown off a shed,
beams bent like matchsticks,
a drove of white cows
making their home
in a derailed train car.

Pottery Lessons I

hokte   hokte   honvnwv*
begin here
with the clay she says
under her breath   a handful of earth
from silt-bottomed streams
loosens between fingers   water
echoes in an empty bowl   hokte
          hoktet hecet os*
I was birthed of mud   blood
And bone   hokte
                  hoktet hecet os
glass globes
inside my tin belly
echo of water
in an empty bowl
I remember the sound of her soft
body   hokte
                  hokte   honvnwv
Have just begun
to bleed today
thought I might be dying
walked barefoot beyond
the backyard
over the cattle guard   hokte
                        hokte   honvnwv
each grass blade
a rusted glint   in the circular
basin of bison
grazing   clay rims
the water colored sky
in the empty bowl
water echoes

---

*Mvskoke (Muscogee)—hokte: woman, honvnwv: man, hecet os: to see

when we walk
horizons shift   how to call them
closer   feel their white tufts
between fingertips   *hokte*

                    hokte   honvnwv

Birthmark

Homeland? On my ankle: claw
or fin. *Mud?* No. I was born with it.
A bit of dirt and I stole it back.
Permanent insertion: under the skin.

Use my frog dissection kit.
Do it in the bathtub so I can hide
the blood. *Blemish: many women have them.*
Homeland. *Cosmetic surgery.*

Scab. *You were born with it.*
Whittling knife: what the women
once used. *You will never know
Grief. Deep,* as if grief were some

body of water. I begin. To teach myself
to swim. Inside a continent.
A scar on my skin.
When the blood dries it looks like

ink. In secret. *She may harm herself
if I send her home.* I travel often
without a map. Found a garden
inside a wall made of river stones.

Bones among the weeds, wild roses,
was not supposed to be there—
running so fast—thorn-scraped ankles.
That's how I got here.

That's what I tell the psychiatrist.
Yes, it looks like a lung. A drawing of a lung
should be enough for them so I decide
to stop speaking. For a month. Keep on forgetting

my name when they ask me.
On purpose, just to please them.
It will be safer for you here
and then you can go home.

What is your language?
Nouns doing something to something

else. *Verb: what you contain*
between them. A place

to pass through until I forget
I had the map of that place
to begin with. Born with it,
a stain on the skin. A garden

always flowering,
petals dropping. With them
I go down rapids.
What is the destination?

Write a letter when I decide to go.
Dear Ghost: Nothing left to say.
I want only to be round again,
rolled between thumbs, a bead

folded back inside the leather
where I come from—*preference*:
writing. With pens.
I learn the names of medications

keep the bird beneath my skin.
This is preservation.
Tell my father: *it is a birthmark*
not a scar.

~

It looks like a little boat to me.
Something to cross by.
I take the knife only because
I want to survive.

Grief is a deep and dreamless creek
until I dream. Drown in my living room
when no one is home. *That's how I got here.*
That's what I tell the psychiatrist.

In the dream it is a claw print of a bird.
Sharp enough to write with.
I put it in my mouth.
What kind of girl are you?

The girl you want me to be. *Be proud
of where you come from.*
Where do birds come from?
The scar fits you. In the same way

Grandmother gives me white gloves:
initiation rite into the first bright day.
I was bleeding up to the eyelids
of the sun, the light in its pillbox:
                    Where do you come from?

I don't see my name
in the provided spelling.
The gloves aren't white
after the garden. Sometimes

skin does not wash clean of earth,
does not replace itself. Sometimes

you have to cut skin deeper
for the wound to heal, to locate
in a different way—running:
find your own map on the body.

Inside it. Carved into passage.
Sometimes you have to drown
to retrieve it from the river-bottom.
Where are you going? Home. Land.

What is your homeland? A framing
of absence, echo of water.
*You will have to live
with these scars now.*

No. I am retracing my name.

Chimera

I have traveled this continent
for no other reason but to search
for evidence of your existence.

In the stars, America, your highway
vanishes. Black moths are captured
in headlights and swallowed.

In the beginning, you had said,
we were cracked against the sky.
Now I read the highway
for the fall-out of your name
as you step again into the passing lane,
turn to the illuminated crest of hill
where a line of traffic outlines the dark—

in your silhouette I can still see myself
as a child, waiting for a car
to swerve around the corner.

But no car came that afternoon.
I stood there in the patient street,
my summer dress rippling.

Blood Moon Triptych

I. PALIMPSEST

We watched the eclipse
under burnt-out street lamps
until we darkened into the same

imprint: bone, tree,
every other breath
one of ocean.

Moon
earth fragment
remember us.

II. ECLIPSE

Time is so demanding
wearing out all the linens—

the parchment, tablets,
my evening melody.

As if the margins
were attempting to cross
the poem, corpse

of the corpus.
Moon's imprinted veil.

III. VEIL

Stumble past cypress
to the cliff's edge—

below you the town's lights
blink—extinguished.

Orion, the giant,
walks blind over water.

What you see in the waves
are not stars: look up!

Bright net cast across
still-frosted pines—

leafy sea dragons,
ballerina eels.

You drift, a planet
forgotten in the infinite

body—dashed
on a soundless stone.

The clot in the sky
is not the moon

but blood—the body
you turned against.

Canyon

Brush over star's dust,
upthrust shale,
erosion-stripped script of ledges—

sloughing scales off
our hands' finned imprints,
slow-aging metamorphic skins
      quartz

          schist

                gypsum—
marine bones bedded in the drainage.

The basin overflows with wind.
Horizon   phantom barges,
a shore once lush with cane.
Moon—a relic in the azure sky,
gray face cut from the mountain's spine.

A line of dust divides us—*narwhal*
& ghost—ancient stream
whose sound remains
      floodland / arroyo

          yucca / saguaro

I dive with pipevine swallowtails
down winding stairs, crenulated lava—
scrolls, fossilized in radiant strata, read
      prickly pear / silver cholla
        spicules of sponge

Here in this rain-shadow's stark
flanked gully, two blue-bellied lizards
streak across sand—vanish
inside a conch shell. *Arrived*
at the bottom of the world, I write.

Buried in the canyon's
spiraled larynx—
      a raft for the coming storm.

NATALIE DIAZ

Natalie Diaz is a Mojave poet and enrolled member of the Gila River Indian Community. Diaz is an indigenous language activist and former professional basketball player. Her honors include a Lannan Literary Fellowship, a US Artist Ford Fellowship, and the Hodder Fellowship at Princeton University.

When My Brother Was an Aztec (2012) is Diaz's first book of poetry. Her next collection is *post-colonial love poem.*

Dome Riddle

Tonight I am riddled by this thick skull

this white bowling ball zipped in the sad-sack carrying case of my face,
this overwound bone jack-in-the-box,
this Orlando's zero, Oaxacan offering: *cabeza locada, calayera azucarada,
        clavo jodido, cenote* of Mnemosyne,
this sticky-sweet guilt hive, *piedra blanca del rio oscuro,*
this small-town medical mania dispensary, prescribed cranium pill,
this electric blue tom-tom drum ticking like an Acme bomb, hypnotized
        explosive device, pensive general, scalp-strapped warrior, soldier
        with a loaded God complex,
this Hotchkiss-obliterated headdress, Gatling-lit labyrinth,
this memory grenade, death epithet, death epitaph, mound of *momento
        mori,*
this twenty-two-part talisman wearing a skirt of breasts, giant ball of
        masa,
this god patella in the long leg of my torso, zoo of canines and Blake's
        tygers,
this red-skinned apple, lamp illuminated by teeth, gang of grin, spitwad
        of scheme,
this jawbone of an ass, smiling sliver of smite, David's rock striking the
        Goliath of my body,
this Library of Babel, homegrown Golgotha, nostalgia menagerie, melon
        festival,
this language mausoleum; *chuksanych iraavtahanm, 'avi kwa'anyay,
        sumach nyamasav,*
this hidden glacier hungry for a taste of titanic flesh,
this pleasure altar, French-kiss sweatshop, abacus of one-night stands,
        hippocampus whorehouse, oubliette of regret,
this church of tongue, chapel of vengeance, cathedral of thought, bone
        dome of despair, *plaza del toro y pensamientos,*

this museum of tribal dentistry, commodity cranium cupboard, petrified
        dream catcher,
this sun-ruined basketball I haul—rotted gray along the seams—perpetual
        missed shot,

this insomnia podium, little bowl in a big fish, brain amphitheater, girl in
    the moon,
this 3 a.m. war bell, *duende* vision prison,
this single-scoop vanilla head rush, thunder head, fastball, lightning rod,
this mad scientist in a white lab helmet, ghost of Smoking Mirror,
this coyote beacon, calcium corral of pale perlino ponies,
this desert seed I am root to, night-blooming cereus, gourd gone rattle,
this Halloween crown, hat rack, worry contraption, Rimbaud's drunken
    boat, blazing chandelier, *casa de relámpago,*
this coliseum *venation:* Borges's other tiger licking the empty shell of
    Lorca's white *tortuga,*
this underdressed godhead, forever-hatching egg, this mug again and
    again at my lips,

and all this because tonight I imagined you sleeping with her
the way we once slept—as intimate as a jaw, maxilla and mandible hot,
in the skin—in love, our heads almost touching.

Other Small Thundering

We are born with spinning coins in place of eyes,
paid in full to ferry Charon's narrow skiffs—
    we red-cloaked captains helming dizzying fits
    of sleep. Tied to the masts,
not to be driven mad by the caroling of thirsty children
or the symphony of dogs slaking hunger
by licking our ribcages like xylophones.
Our medicine bags are anchored with buffalo nickels—
    sleek skulls etched by Gatlings.
How we plow and furrow the murky Styx, lovingly
digging with smooth dark oars—
    like they are Grandmother's missing legs—
        a familiar throb of kneecap, shin, ankle, foot—
    promising to carry us home.

A gunnysack full of tigers wrestles in our chests—
    they pace, stalking our hearts, building a jail
    with their stripes. Each tail a fuse. Each eye a cinder.
Chest translates to bomb.
Bomb is a song—
    the drum's shame-hollowed lament.
Burlap is no place for prayers or hands.
The reservation is no place for a jungle.
    But our stomachs growl. Somewhere within us
    there lies a king, and when we find him . . .

The snow-dim prairies are garlanded with children—
    my people fancy dance circles around pyres but do not
    celebrate the bodies, small, open, red as hollyhocks.
Some crawled until they came undone—
    petal by petal,
    striping the white field crimson.
Others lay where they first fell, enamored by the warmth
Of a blanket of blood.

My dress is bluer than a sky weeping bones—
    so this is the way to build a flag—
        with a pretty little Springfield .45 caliber rifle.
    So this is the way to sew wounds—
        with a hot little Howitzer.

Yesterday is much closer than today—
    a black bayonet carried between the shoulder blades
    like an itch or the bud of a wing.
We've memorized the way a Hotchkiss can wreck a mouth.
Streetlights glow, neon gourds, electric dandelions—
    blow them out!
Wish hard for orange buttes and purple canyons,
moon-hoofed horses with manes made from wars,
other small thundering.

American Arithmetic

Native Americans make up less than
one percent of the population of America.
0.8 percent of 100 percent.

O, mine efficient country.

I do not remember the days
before America—I do not remember the days
when we were all here.

Police kill Native Americans more
than any other race. *Race* is a funny word
Race implies someone will win,
implies *I have as good a chance of winning as*—

Who wins the race which isn't a race?

Native Americans make up 1.9 percent
of all police killings, higher than any race,
and we exist as .8 percent of all Americans.

Sometimes *race* means *run*.

We are not good at math.
Can you blame us?
We've had an American education.

We are Americans and we are less than 1 percent
of Americans. We do a better job of dying
by police than we do existing.

When we are dying, who should we call?
The police? Or our senator?
Please, someone, call my mother.

In Arithmetic and in America,
divisibility has rules—
divide without remainder.

At the National Museum of the American Indian,

68 percent of the collection is from the U.S.
I am doing my best to not become a museum
of myself. I am doing my best to breathe in and out.

I am begging: *Let me be lonely but not invisible.*

But in this American city with all its people,
I am Native American—less than one, less than
whole—I am less than myself. Only a fraction
of a body, let's say, *I am only a hand—*

and when I slip it beneath the shirt of my lover
I disappear completely.

The First Water Is the Body

The Colorado River is the most endangered river in the United States—also, it is a part of my body.

I carry a river. It is who I am: *'Aha Makav.*

This is not metaphor.

When a Mojave says, *Inyech 'Aha Makavch ithuum,* we are saying our name. We are telling a story of our existence. *The river runs through the middle of my body.*

So far, I have said the word *river* in every stanza. I don't want to waste water. I must preserve the river in my body.

In future stanzas, I will try to be more conservative.

~

The Spanish called us, *Mojave. Colorado,* the name they gave our river because it was silt-red-thick.

Natives have been called *red* forever. I have never met a red native, not even on my reservation, not even at the Museum of the American Indian, not even at the largest powwow in Parker, Arizona.

I live in the desert along a dammed blue river. The only red people I've seen are white tourists sunburned after being out on the water too long.

~

'Aha Makav is the true name of our people, given to us by our Creator who loosed the river from the earth and built it, into our living bodies.

Translated into English, *'Aha Makav* means *the river runs through the middle of our body, the same way it runs through the middle of our land.*

This is a poor translation, like all translations.

In American minds, the logic of this image will lend itself to surrealism or magical realism—

Americans prefer a magical red Indian, or a shaman, or a fake Indian in a red dress, over a real native. Even a real native carrying the dangerous and heavy blues of a river in her body.

What threatens white people is often dismissed as myth.
I have never been true in America. America is my myth.

~

Derrida says, *Every text remains in mourning until it is translated.*

When Mojaves say the word for *tears*, we return to our word for *river*, as if our river were flowing from our eyes. *A great weeping*, is how you might translate it. Or, *a river of grief.*

But who is this translation for? And will they come to my language's four-night funeral to grieve what has been lost in my efforts at translation? When they have drunk dry my river will they join the mourning procession across our bleached desert?

The word for *drought* is different across many languages and lands.

The ache of thirst, though, translates to all bodies along the same paths— the tongue and the throat. No matter what language you speak, no matter the color of your skin.

~

We carry the river, its body of water, in our body.

I do not mean to imply a visual relationship. Such as:—a native woman on her knees holding a box of Land O' Lakes butter whose label has a picture of a native woman on her knees holding a box of Land O' Lakes butter whose label has a picture of a native woman on her knees . . .

We carry the river, its body of water, in our body. I do not mean to invoke the Droste effect.

I mean *river* as a verb. A happening. It is moving within me right now.

~

This is not juxtaposition. Body and water are not *two unlike things*—they are more than *close together or side by side.* They are *same*—body, being, energy, prayer, current, motion, medicine.

This knowing comes from acknowledging the human body has more than six senses. The body is beyond six senses. Is sensual. Is always an ecstatic state of energy, is always on the verge of praying, or entering any river of movement.

Energy is a moving like a river moving my moving body.

~

In Mojave thinking, body and land are the same. The words are separated only by letters: 'iimat for body, 'amat for land. In conversation, we often use a shortened form for each: mat-. Unless you know the context of a conversation, you might not know if we are speaking about our body or our land. You might not know which has been injured, which is remembering, which is alive, which was dreamed, which needs care, which has vanished.

If I say, *My river is disappearing,* do I also mean, *My people are disappearing?*

~

How can I translate—not in words but in belief—that a river is a body, as alive as you or I, that there can be no life without it?

~

John Berger wrote, "true translation is not a binary affair between two languages but a triangular affair. The third point of the triangle being what lay behind the words of the original text before it was written. True translation demands a return to the pre-verbal."

Between the English translation I offered, and the urging I felt to first type *'Aha Makav* in the lines above, is not the point where this story ends or begins.

We must go to the place before those two points—we must go to the third place that is the river.

We must go to the point of the lance our creator stabbed into the earth, and the first river bursting from that clay body into mine. We must submerge beneath those once warm red waters now channeled-blue and cool, the current's endless yards of emerald silk wrapping the body and moving it, swift enough to take life or give it.

We must go until we smell the black-root-wet anchoring the river's mud banks.

~

What is this third point, this place beyond the surface, if not the deep-cut and crooked bone bed where the Colorado River runs—like a one thousand four-hundred and fifty mile thirst—into and through a body?

Berger called it the *pre-verbal*. *Pre-verbal* as in the body when the body was more than body. Before it could name itself *body* and be limited to the space *body* indicated.

Pre-verbal is the place where the body was yet a green-blue energy greening, greened and bluing the stone, the floodwaters, the razorback fish, the beetle, and the cottonwoods' and willows' shaded shadows.

Pre-verbal was when the body was more than a body and possible.

One of its possibilities was to hold a river within it.

~

A river is a body of water. It has a foot, an elbow, a mouth. It runs. It lies in a bed. It can make you good. It remembers everything.

~

America is a land of bad math and science: the Right believes Rapture will save them from the violence they are delivering upon the earth and water; the Left believes technology, the same technology wrecking the earth and water, will save them from the wreckage or help them build a new world on Mars.

~

If I was created to hold the Colorado River, to carry its rushing inside me, how can I say who I am if the river is gone?

What does 'Aha Makav mean if the river is emptied to the skeleton of its fish and the miniature sand dunes of its dry silten beds?

If the river is a ghost, am I?

Unsoothable thirst is one type of haunting.

~

A phrase popular or more known to non-natives during the Standing Rock encampment was, Water is the first medicine. It is true.

Where I come from we cleanse ourselves in the river. Not like a bath with soap. I mean: the water makes us strong and able to move forward into what is set before us to do with good energy.

We cannot live good, we cannot live at all, without water.

If we poison and use up our water, how will we cleanse ourselves of these sins?

~

To thirst and to drink is how one knows they are alive, and grateful.

To thirst and then not drink is . . .

~

If your builder could place a small red bird in your chest to beat as your heart, is it so hard for you to picture the blue river hurtling inside the slow muscled curves of my long body? Is it too difficult to believe it is as sacred as a breath or a star or a sidewinder or your own mother or your lover?

If I could convince you, would our brown bodies and our blue rivers be more loved and less ruined?

The Whanganui river in New Zealand now has the same legal rights of a human being. In India, the Ganges and Yamuna rivers now have the same legal status of a human being. Slovenia's constitution now declares access to clean drinking water to be a national human right. While in the U.S., we are tear-gassing and rubber-bulleting and kenneling natives trying to protect their water from pollution and contamination at Standing Rock in North Dakota. We have yet to discover what the effects of lead contaminated water will be on the children of Flint, Michigan who have been drinking it for years.

~

We think of our bodies as being all that we are: *I am my body*. This thinking helps us disrespect water, air, land, one another. But water is not external from our body, our self.

My Elder says: *Cut off your ear, and you will live. Cut off your hand, you will live. Cut off your leg, you can still live. Cut off our water: we will not live more than a week.*

The water we drink, like the air we breathe, is not a part of our body but is our body. What we do to one—to the body, to the water—we do to the other.

~

Toni Morrison writes, *All water has a perfect memory and is forever trying to get back to where it was.* Back to the body of earth, of flesh, back to the mouth, the throat, back to the womb, back to the heart, to its blood, back to our grief, back back back to when we were more than we have lately become.

Will we soon remember from where we've come? The water.

And once remembered, will we return to that first water, and in doing so return to ourselves, to each other, better and cleaner?

Do you think the water will forget what we have done, what we continue to do?

TREVINO L. BRINGS PLENTY

Trevino L. Brings Plenty was born on the Cheyenne River Sioux Reservation, Eagle Butte, South Dakota. A Minneconjou Lakota, he grew up in the San Francisco Bay area and Portland, Oregon, where he now resides. Brings Plenty is a filmmaker and musician, and has been a social worker, college instructor, and advocate for Native families and students.

Real Indian Junk Jewelry (2012) is Brings Plenty's first poetry collection. He has since published *Wakpa Wanagi Ghost River* (2015).

For the Sake of Beauty

On the phone I asked her to wear a full buckskin outfit and she could be the beauty that would make me steal horses.

She said she didn't have a buckskin outfit.

I said I would make her one, but use pages from books.

A week later when she came over to my place, she asked if I had made an outfit.

I said no. I couldn't bring myself to hunt the books on my shelf, even if it were for food or clothing. I couldn't bring myself to kill, even for the sake of beauty.

The Sound of It

When you spoke of it you sounded the explosion, the skyline, love's water rush, the wilted fist, the scream of a desert, the cracked moon, and oblivion's color. You spoke of the dark, blue night around my eyes.

Part Gravel, Part Water, All Indian

It's not by accident
I live in a city.

It was calculated:
a bloodline of misery,

a nonwhite skin,
a tongue not made for English,

years to germinate genocidal loss.
I live to wait as anybody else

not for handouts,
but hand-me-down lives:

work boots, white T-shirts, blue jeans.
I am the Other of this

American Other masked in common clothes.
My homeland is occupied by debt.

My language is not in my dreams.
My heart is ripped to shreds.

My lungs burn with fire/smoke.
My body is diseased by civilization.

My mind is a nomadic madness.
I live where concrete sterilizes life.

Blizzard South Dakota

Months afterwards, I see the electrical poles
piled along the road.

When the blizzard smothered the land,
my tribe was displaced.
Like shot gun blasts heard in the distance,
those poles snapped,
weighted by ice.

A month in motels,
we ate fast food,
while the winter deer meat
expired in the basement.

Movie stars flocked to Haiti.
We watched the news,
wondered about us,
about our reservation,
about our home.

Those dialysis machines failed
without electricity,
pushed people farther away,
closer to the spirit world.

I still hear those poles
ricochet at these wakes.

Northeast Portland

In seeing a woman weep on her doorstep
the loss of her children
to child welfare for a second time
and knowing the difficult road
yet to navigate, my brain maps crisis.

My brain foretells her children
penetrating deep into the system
and her grandchildren
entering the system; my brain maps crisis.

This is the second time for this mother,
in this state, that her children were removed
There is her home rez where
her other children are placed elsewhere.
She pines returning home. Some safety.
Her father lives there; my brain maps crisis.

I can only offer a few words
of encouragement and support,
suggest consult her doctor for med adjustments;
make required appointments and supervised visits,
try not to break down.
My brain wanders elsewhere
to a friend on the borderline
of disenrollment from her tribe.
I think liquid identity
scalping extermination: my brain maps crisis.

I return to my car. Start the engine,
power on the radio—the static feels
comforting. I drive this city, see tornadoes
in households. I can point out
people's pain traced across streets,
the many histories of removal:
socio-economic, racial, generational
mental health states. My brain maps crisis.

Not Just Anybody Can Have One

So, I'll use my tribal enrollment until it disappears. Until I'm kicked out of my tribe for questioning the motives of nepotism; until the US government makes policy change. Until there is enough rumor to make it true.

My tribal enrollment was designed by/for imprisonment. A generational countdown to oblivion. It is the Holy Grail for some when they are in search of a culture to make sense of fire in their life; to prove others wrong and themselves valid.

Like anything else assigned, it is developed to be a certain outcome. In its language are the shackles of enforcement. Enrollment is in fear of dis-enrollment. We wait for grass from fracked resources and water's structure forever transfigured. We wait because what is said is never followed through. There are branches holding bits of sky, its leaves coated with stardust and bird shit. There are cliffs carved with horse hooves and porcupine hair; lakes cultivating cancers; wells drugged by disaster.

I insert my tribal identification card into ATMs to withdraw my ancestors' blood. Vials and packets to sustain the slaughter. Every day cloaked in night, I weather my granite bones through wood and concrete. I dare this fair city and its peoples no harm other than what story has transpired. This place lit by memory. The epigenetic invasion masked as peaceful dialogue.

Red-ish Brown-ish

Arms, face, scrotum—dark brown.
The kind of brown to drive
monsters to exterminate
bison to starve
a people.

Design policy with intentional marketing titles.
Assimilation; Relocation; Termination.
Enough to talk about a vanishing race
in front of you as theory and practice.
Enough to throw stats out
as a summation of cultural identity.

Erasure thread of empire
its subjects uneasy,
comfort
to express you as object.

And to say it's just conver-
sation. Or playing devil's ad-
vocate. Maybe they know
closed fists in pockets
they change subject.

I use shading—the back of hands
to gauge who is in the tutelage
of systemic beauty.
Adorned, beautiful works so well.

Ripe for violence, I carry lived stories
interface beauteous facade.
Have seen coil unravel belly at day's end.
My social media feed curiosity curated
reinforced by other agenda.
It's barbed threading through digits.
I work through the other's language,
I feel hypocritical. I dream English language.

Plasmic Kiln

Broken TV console base, tube TV seated. Burnt.
La-Z-Boy, green love seat, green couch. Burnt.
Yellow, brown shag carpet, wood paneling, pink Formica tops. Burnt.
Coat rack, white wooden dresser, shoes by door. Burnt.
Stereo system, large speakers, record collection. Burnt.
Queen bed, twin beds, crib, cot. Burnt.

The dog cleared a den under the back door cement stair. Neighbor kid ignited the hay filling. The house burnt down.

The lone survivor, I was blamed, orphaned by flame. At five years young, I couldn't understand how to start a fire when not present.

My face fragments in those charred kin. In candid photos of me smiling, I see grandma's nose, cheeks. My mother's eyes, father's lips, grandfather's chin and hairline. The veins under the meaty part of my palm—is this sibling?

To every room entered,
        ghostly flame spill across floor.
                Plastic, wood, flesh perfume air.

Minding corridors blaze,
        solar flare through body.
                Lamps puddle. Heat is light—sensation form.

The fingers, flames scraping back.
        Human in dance. Bones prostrated
                on metal bed springs. Ash layer nose lining.

Song Syntax Cycle

Refresh rate is per generation pixelated words

sung from cavernous throats.

Masticate titles. Interface analog substance . . .

There is no sine wave.

Device shapes hand, navigates digits.

Sunlit face contour splays hand print across wall.

#OneDotAmongMany

#SoEasyToHideBodies

#DigitalHaunting

~

Swarm buzz in head, "attempts," red soaked towels,
children moved to other rooms. Out of eyesight.
Trace episode gushed out.

Medication refusal, convincing them to drop knife
at last crisis. Let there be space while weeping at
dining room table.

So casual—the incidents unravel in dark rooms,
stoke them alive. Three generations stitched to-
gether in HUD home.

Back of eyes hurt—shells grinding sand.
Thunder storm heavy and dank in air.

(A young girl seated on floor. Electrical cord. She
would pass out before anything happened. We wait.)

Think of a time river swimming—orange noon heat. A favorite thing to do. Same location relatives washed ashore. Bloated body. It's scary when they go missing. It's scarier when they return.

Pulls down eyeglasses, blows nose. Face is flushed. Begin to draft safety plan. Script best case scenarios. No successful exit discussion.

~

Trauma halos in midstream, the conversations coveted.

Concrete pushed us closer to light emitting diodes strung drunkenly across town's neck.

Dark eyes sunk deep. Dark matter history supernova colossal loss without end. One enveloped the other, thrashed across body.

Interior mothers—places visited to deconstruct ladders stacked in emotional torrents, currents and streams occupied skull attics.

So much danger in hands. Fear they influence children's instruction. Absolution distilled, white of eyes. Crushed many without recourse. Maybe they not I have done more damage.

Tell more of north, solar flares shaving the atmosphere. Bent eyelids, singular horizon circumference. Say it burned. Say this pretty thing out of its element is love scorched. Not a scavenger's meal.

~

There among bone-white notes

     Heated rock liquid into ocean

     Hands dip into sand

Sing equator, bloated dialects fissure this earth-based trajectory

All its equations webbed—the tongue shaped by meaning

     Objects sentient to their course

     Close eyes, believe it dark matter

Watch absence inverted

dg nanouk okpik

dg nanouk okpik is Inupiaq-Inuit, raised in Anchorage, Alaska. She has earned an AFA from Salish Kootenai College in liberal arts/liberal studies, a BFA at the Institute of American Indian Arts, and an MFA at the University of Southern Maine's Stonecoast College. Her first book is winner of the American Book Award. dg nanouk okpik works for the Museum of Indian Arts and Culture/Laboratory of Anthropology in Santa Fe with high-risk native students teaching poetry as a healing art.

Corpse Whale (2012) is okpik's first full-length poetry collection. Her next collection is *Thaw*.

Warming

She and I make a bladder bag to draw water from the ice trench.
She/I chain stitch/es a skin dressed in oil to make a new pot of soup.
She/I sew/s a badger hair rough around the top of her/my *kamiks*
to make the steps windward, toward the limits of woman.
She/I eat/s club root and white clover to strengthen her/my silver
body to bear a child. She/I map/s, following 1 degree from the North
Star and 60 degrees from the end of the earth's axis on rotation
for *Ukpeagvik* she/I use/s a small arc of ice, cleaving into parts, reduced
to simple curves fitted with serrated edges of white flesh. She/I mold/s
to the fretted neck of frozen water into a deep urn, made like a
     rock shelter
or a cavern. She/I construct/s a hole on the surface of a glacier formed
     by melting particles
of roc and pan reservoir dust from a shelter for the ice worms. Because
     the earth is
molding, burning, laughing, and purging its crust.

Her/My Arctic
 Corpse Whale

It comes back to the Inuit me:
images   in the mirror are closer   than they appear

on my kayak skin boat.   She/I was forged by sea salt
by snow   hammered   into iron ore   red herring.

While she's/I'm paddling   another floating corpse,
a spotted human peltgloos   a narwhal is passing
                    a turquoise iceberg.
Of plucked   bones of ivory   with spiral blood   stained ribbons

reduced   to a single   tusk. She/I pass/es,   and keep/s paddling,
in a sea with gray   and choppy   scarlet walls of water.

Our carnage fuel oil   wicks in lighted igloos
on polar seaboard   next to washed up
empty   blue-green coke bottle   fishing floats,
floats   mark a thread   bare seine net   packed with arms

            of purple octopus   grabbing the rearview mirrors.
                                She/I keep/s paddling.

Towing a nine-foot tusk   draggle   a blood trail,

gaff the glass and blink. The eyelids   shun risky   long-handed

Braille   rope: pacts.   Her/my eardrums playing   an
old throat song,
dry as sunspots.
                    She/I keep/s paddling.

In a lidless cesarean section   of ozone layer   is a white giant
looks through   a tainted glass rope porthole

adopts young Inuit   like mottled jellyfish, suck
blood quantum   and raises underground   flags beneath Polaris Star
        She/I keep/s paddling.

Her/my flouncing caribou   in dark moonlight are dodging   Bush laws.

Her/my Malamute   trots in Arctic circles
before the midnight   storm.
Her/my ringed seal barks   couplets of foreshadows   in an oval
tasting

room
with white columns and musty   yellowed law books.
She/I keep/s paddling

Reaching the shore   of the Beaufort Sea landing the kayak

She/I witness/es in triple-thick   permafrost of sea   and land merging,
the Inuit skeletons are rising like brittle   driftwood ivory
as the Stellar Eagle   plummets and she/I try/ies pushing,

pushing, and shoving   the sinew back   into the threaded
                        bones of the land.

The Weight of the Arch Distributes the Girth of the Other

If she/I maneuver/s   with the new moon— her/my shadow-shadow/s

shift   to the dark side,   hold   her/my distended
stomach/s   if she/I watch/es him   shape change in the
        morning hours   will the weight   of the arch shift?
            The adoption is final. The girl raven is beautiful and round.
                    Envisage the bestial nature of man,
            summon an innate mother's love for her new girl part raven.
As a hound pines   to be a wolf   a rosary prayer string

Made of snowberry seeds severs her wrist.   See a small ray unlock
                                        the namesake

in soft gleams of   light circumscribed   by dry root in   the other.
Killbear.
She/I=daughter=namesake=Killbear from Wainwright not far from
        Barrow=raven woman.

A Year Dot

FOR ARTHUR SZE

(Qin) Dim Sum equivalent to: *dot, speck heart*

Stone piled on stone I finish my meal.
In this early sunrise I see shadows where a cairn of rocks
used to stack in the direction of eastern light.

In late morning, I lit red candles and placed them
next to a three-hinged mirror, as a way of seeing
shadows of shadows

Milkweed grows on the side of the road in ditches,
reminiscent of professor's soft words, amazing the brilliant,
contemplation and thought pattern as you learn, slowly.

In my body neuron-zipped words and more words.
My lexicon building from nothing to something good.
Embossed tattoos like small notes on sheet music.

Dots and lines, strands and strings I rest on the note D,
Increased by one half as my orchestra director signals,
dashes and spaces for letters as grace notes in Morse code.

Notes in staccato igniting instrumental waves of burning wood,
a fiery spark over and speck dust played in harmonics,
as a cool hovers over a brook dives in comes back with a fish.

No one would ever know its true beauty and calmness
the setting sun across an arctic lake unless it is witnessed.
As speckled day owls, brants and mergansers float in the sunset.

To learn you must be open, diligent, and willing to be an individual.
11,000 murres with webbed feet land also without any fear of predators.
But still, on the page grow spotted mushrooms and morrels.

Examine the distortion and effects of the warming earth.
The change of the ice age with purpose as the warming earth today,
But I take heart in sun along with the core of a gingko trees light.

Dog Moon Night at Noatak

A dog moon winter night,
in frigid, crackled, dry, ice
an old weathered man mushed,
The sled knows north of the crested bergs
Many runs his dog team raced with tongues
hanging red with dripping saliva,
each paw bleeding from the sliced
new wet melt.

In a cobalt blue snow scape how
frightening the illness came on.
How the brittle glass cracked slightly
askew in a roar of pieces as the permafrost,
sank flat and collapsed under paw, and feet.
It's then I passed out in the cocooned basket.

In sledge a fever broke with a dry
hoarse cry of stomach pain. We went.
My goose-feathered flesh indigo,
his face pale but red at the cheekbones.
yet shiny from the hoarfrost sweat like
the needles pricking the ice as it bleeds.

When is cold   cold? Are we there yet?
When is rain   rain?   Does it matter to many?
What's left   behind or ahead? As now approaches.

Cold is warm sometimes like   hear and now.
I turn frost bitten daily not from blue biting pike fish
but from the light rain at 300 miles north of the arctic
circle. It's always in flux-flow like quarks slamming
in quantum mechanics. At the opened slush and sky melt
I awaken to a tree of palms and cactus spines in Noatak.
I gaze up, view the dog moon in silence, and shiver.

She Travels

Time as a Japanese coke bottle float
                              bobbing the ocean surface

Anywhere   but on the shore of Kivalina.

        A number as time is labeled
It reads: *parallelism is not a question but a space   here*

I am a   woman of time   a worm hole vacuum
I travel every 4 days   on a walkabout

Between two events   one 10,923 days ago
        one: here & now

                      now   using the speed of light
        a glow spark casting off in the solar dust

I like to wander   to find things
                                a pretty rock
                                a shell
                                a slice of baleen

On this shoreline   in this time   here in a karigi
            A \ceremonial dance for snow
I carry a clock watch round my head in a locket
I carry light in my feet   shine step into this place

I see an acrobatic lady of the plants she gives me medicine
In her DNA she preprogrammed with 2117 of seed knowledge

Her carved microcrystalline murmurs through   this taiga
She is named Old Squaw Duck   tossed and tumbled   now   here
        at a   blanket toss
                      in Kivalina

JULIAN TALAMANTEZ BROLASKI

Julian Talamantez Brolaski, mixed Lipan and Mescalero Apache, is the author of and coeditor of *NO GENDER: Reflections on the Life & Work of kari edwards* (2009). Julian sings with the Bay Area American Indian Two-Spirits drum and is the lead singer and rhythm guitarist in the country bands Juan & the Pines (New York City) and the Western Skyline (Oakland).

Brolaski's first poetry collection is *gowanus atropolis* (2011), and he has since published *Advice for Lovers* (2012) and *Of Mongrelitude* (2017).

Blackwater Stole My Pronoun

abysse in fr. referes to the sea specifically
as opposed to a crevasse on land
how we say the grand canyon
or credit ratings are abysmal

one can be in abi^me, complete ruin
as jwlhyfer observed
once you start fucking in the bed
the relationship's over

blackwater stole my pronoun
as February unclenches its fist
like hitler using 卍
like martial's plagiarius

In the Cut

FOR CEDAR SIGO

> *his being punished / for talking Indian.*
> —Cedar Sigo, "Prince Valiant"

person of clear salt water
warm clear deer

the mosquitoes I am
delicious to them
because of my fairy
or my indian blood

he is immune
to poison ivy
because indians dont
call it poison

utter unfaith in humanity
the leaves dont turn right
the leaves so that
they dont know how to turn right

when the guy at the bodega
complained about white ppl & gentrifications
you said me and my friend are native
I'm Suquamish, look it up

I vaporize the weed
we had for breakfast when
I come home from the poetry reading
thinking how low & how lively
we know of the cut

droppd my parasol in a ditch
pretend it didnt happen

What Do They Know of Suffering,
Who Eat of Pineapples Yearround

Lrsn, brute battlements of infamy cd not
nor the former planet pluto, nor even those
pulchritudinous characters who scape
even usen's reach, the plumes, nor yet
those fruits who are bred to be
of uniform size, watermelons squard
compliant papayas, I followed the norteñəs
train to train, the field populates or the field
was filled—what do they know of suffering
who eat of pineapples yearround?
& the edifices tho they enscrape the sky
were not so near as high as we
down by that ridiculous stream,
whos dappled mere the better part of me
but if we make this our last moorings
it were no burthen to me, friend
who attend yr company this day

As the Owl Augurs

FOR INÉS TALAMANTEZ

I have an hour to read marcabru and fall in love
to study the medicines and put a rock in each corner of the house
and pray over it with pollen as my elder advised
to test my unextraordinary knowledgeses
to briefly wonder whether I was actually under a spell
to write my poem about being a mongrel
I must love even the fox that impedes my path
n jettison my former ire n any gesture toward abstraction
n go to the dump finally w/ the disused bicycle tires and the broken
    antlers and the cracked stained glass of a ship that formerly I wdve
    harbored because I did not love myself
but the broken shelf
I want namore of it
the jangle-mongrel and the rose and the ndn cowboy that layall closeted
along w/ my availablility to my own mind and the killings of our
    familyes queer and black and brown and ndn
slaughter at orlando symbol of our hermitude
massacre at aravaipa gashdla'á cho o'aa big sycamore standing there
bear river sand creek tulsa rosewood
n when I finally sussed them out
n laid the tequila in its proper trash
n attempted to corral the pony of my mind
they say the ohlone were here as if
there were no more ohlone
erected a fake shellmound called it shellmound avenue
my friends dont like that
my friends dont like that excrement
it's not like youd give away the algorithm, my bf pointed out,
to the one yr tryin to put a spell on
marcabru uses the word 'mestissa' to describe the shepherdess his dickish
    narrator is poorly courting
which paden translates 'half-breed' and pound 'low-born' and
    snodgrass 'lassie' but I want to say mongrel, mestiza, mixedbreed
melissima most honeyed most songful

what catullus called his boyfriend's eyes
honey the color of my dead dog's eyes the stomach of the bee
I'm going to gather pollen from the cattails in a week or two
to pray to the the plant tell it I'm only taking what I need
use a coathanger to hook the ones far from shore
filter it thru chiffon four times
what is love
but a constellation of significances
lyke-like magic
los cavecs noa aüra as the owl augurs
one gapes at a painting
the other waits for mahana

Stonewall to Standing Rock

who by the time it arrived
had made its plan heretofore
stonewall   it had not a penny
thats not true it had several pennies

can you make a sovereign nation a national park how condescending
instead just tell them to honor the treaty

what can poetry do it
cant not not do nothing
it must undulate w/ the 2:30 pm dance music the sole
patrons at stonewall

there was a shooting in ohio today
the music made me feel a little anxious it was
hard thumping dance music a notch
upwards of 100 bpm notoriously the beat of life
the optimum tempo for cpr
I consider downloading a metronome real quick to test it to tap it out but
I don't want to be 'anywhere near' my phone
meaning it's in my bag on the stool 2 feet from me

there is an amy winehouse video on no sound at least
I think it is amy winehouse
she is at a funeral black and white
there is a stuffed bird slightly obscuring my view of the tv
it looks like a kind of tall pigeon w/ mottled brown
and russet with a white ringlet necklace and black dots
is it a carrier pigeon I wonder I sent
a text to jocelyn at standing rock several texts

are you still on the road
ariana and i r gonna go out there in december
sending love to you
tried calling bt yr mailbox is full
send a sign when u can xoxo

howdy. thinking of u w love.
hope all is well. send smoke
signal telegram carrier pigeon
send love to my twospirits at the
winyan camp.

last night we prayed for her and for zephyr and l. frank &
the twospirits especially at standing rock
there's no sign of that struggle here but they are selling tshirts
    commemorating
the other and the six days of riots
led by transwomen of color they later tried to whitewash in that
    terrible movie
like it was all these hot angry upright downright forthright white gays
    so ready
for the revolution
and now people are treating standing rock like burning man

a drink called goslings
videos by the pigeon misaligned with the music
the smell of booze in the air made both of us recoil slightly I saw
or felt it

I'm here to make a poem I was already paid for when I had less than $2 in
my bank account (and I joked I would go right to the bar and buy every-
body drinks) not even enough for a subway ride and I used the 58 cents I'd
gotten for busking for the first time alone in the long hallway between the
library at bryant park and the orange line trains by the ovid quote 'gutta
cavat lapidem' water (or a drop of water really) hollows out
a stone. lapidum a stone or rock ariana once described cd wright's style
    as 'lapidary'
I loved this as a description of writing like the hieroglyphics are
literally lapidary and I told my grandmother about it as we
were driving from mescalero to albuquerque she knew all about the
plants and the names for all the rockforms mesas or buttes or
ziggurats and I said how do

you know all these she said by long observation and
I used to study geology in college I wanted to major in it
but they wouldn't allow women
to major in the hard sciences then so she
began to study religion
tho she already had medicine

ricky martin on the beach
or is it someone younger sexier
the grand canyon splitting apart
is it an ad is it a video
even the sands at the beach
are bouncing with the beat
the tempo has stayed very similar this whole time a tick
up I suspect from 100 bpm

Horse Vision

clock reads 7 at all hours
juncos make selves known in the snow
this time dawdling
I write in horse, but I see in athapaskan
when it's time for elevensies, the clock reads 7
what telling fortune therewith
time is a thing that gets spent, like youth, $ and desire
n/t so lovely as a cardinal against the snow
or a tree w/ fruit on it
by the time I have ceased to write this
it will already be 7
adjourned to the park
n/thing will come of n/t
starfish creak inna wood
lurid amulet   w/ a fish onnit
sign reads SEVEN all day & at all hours
the dogs curse each other from afar
in dog language
when did the word *corrupt* begin to take on a moral cast?
horses see in wide angle, and have a much wider periphery than humans,
but with a blind spot in the very center
so if you want to be sympathetic to a horse say sucks
about those blinders
or if you want to make fun of a horse, tell them
they can't even see whats in front of their fucking face

The Bear and the Salmon

it lyked to eat salmon w/ its
fingers like a bear
and then use those fingers
to clean its glasses
it cried and it looked like a raccoon I believe
it wanted to cultivate this look

When It Rains It Pours

when it rains it pours
the rain it raineth everyday
pull up the reins, rayned in by reason, rule, and reverence
if the aim is total abject embarrassment
of shiny looking objects tenderly gathered for the pome's
sunset quinciñera
a star winked at me btwn the apricot and the cypress
2 crows atop them like a punter on the mizzenmast
u better step up your game, havelok
by what means of studye and devocyon
what is love but a constellation
of significances
it liked to eat salmon w its fingers like a bear
and then use those
fingers to clean its glasses
it cries and it looks like a wolf I believe it wanted
to cultivate this look

The Bear Was Born

the bear was born
thrown from its side by killer-of-enemies
its rage scratched open several rivers and the gulf of mexico
an aspect so to speke
made fulsomely as it were one
whos habitat
full somely made
reaches all its leaves and feathers to the smoky air
a tanager on an elm in oahu
is really reminded of the grand canyon
by the souvenir mug of the muleskinner
& the horse & the name ANGEL

SY HOAHWAH

Sy Hoahwah is Yappithuka Comanche/Southern Arapahoe. He has lived throughout Oklahoma and the southern United States. He holds an MFA in creative writing from the University of Arkansas. He is a recipient of a National Endowment for the Arts Literature Fellowship.

Velroy and the Madischie Mafia (2009) is Hoahwah's first poetry collection. He has since published a chapbook, *Night Cradle* (2011). His next collection, *Ancestral Demon of a Grieving Bride*, is forthcoming.

Anchor-Screws of Culture

After watching the deceased
Comanche Nation Princess
get snagged on an anchor-screw
as she crawled out of the mausoleum,

The first groundskeeper
retrieved a pair of hedge clippers,
but was chased by a swarm of bees in the shape of a big hand.

Second groundskeeper
brandished his brand new cordless drill.
He just had a birthday.

Third groundskeeper
quickly made the oil and gasoline mixture
for the weed-eaters.

Fourth groundskeeper
put out his cigarette
on the back of a concrete lamb.

And the fifth groundskeeper
hooked up water hoses, but stopped to help
a spider loosen its fangs from an empty grasshopper.

The clouds went by
like a Two-Step dance.
Instantly, I fell in love
with the Comanche culture all over again.

Toward Mount Scott

Toward Mount Scott
it is sharp as a knife.

The bad roads lead to lost roads.
The lost roads lead to the same

empty spot. People sometimes go
to lonely places for power.

Eagles are sometimes choked,
dragonflies lassoed.

Smaller birds follow ghosts
to eat off the bugs.

Line of barbed wire
marks the boundary

between this world
and the next.

Ever Since I Can Remember

Ever since I can remember
the decapitated head sings

about being
in a brass bucket

at the foot of a cold mountain.
Then it chases us—

lightning
tied to its hair

jagged teeth glow.
Voice sharpened

on the stones
swallowed.

Speed up
slow down

a vengeance
old tribal times.

What is Left

What is left

of my family's 160 acres:
A lone pecan tree
on the fringe of Cache Creek

A squirrel runs up and down
the trunk

carrying insults

between my dead grandfather
and the birds that live

in the top branches.

I carve my name
on the moon's teeth.

Before We Are Eaten

Before we are eaten,
the raccoon-witch-cannibal-monk sings to us,
showing rolls upon rolls of teeth.

The songs are always about the Arapaho girl
whose parents' names are White Crazy and Grief
and how she offers her last finger as a sacrifice.

Then the cannibal monk takes a bow,
wearing his own gigantic scrotum as a robe.

At the center of the center of the center of things,
he keeps us. His stomach is a small bedroom
with an old mattress and wooden floor

lined with old newspapers
and coffee cans full of kerosene
for the scorpions that come out to mock.

Glitter

My sinister-bent laugh descends
into its own smirk of fire,

and the smoke follows the most beautiful.

The Great Magnet
points the iron in my blood
towards the woods.

I dry-fit moonlight to the openings
Of my fox skull.
It is a church of hunger.

The hunted unfold the wilderness
from their hearts.

I follow . . .
these are walking-alone stars.

Their glitter, I devour
when these apostle-bodies
are charged with the word.

The rest, a mouthful of feathers
spat out over the mountains.

Hinterlands

My ancestors were not diligent
and so they lived beside the fort
that's neither on the maps of Heaven,
Nor of Hell.
In these lands, there is no difference
between a star and thrown car keys.
Chicken nuggets hatch from the eggs of eagles.
I grow dirty while bathing in bottled water.
My bed comforter is a wet parking lot,
I wrap myself up in.
If I eat in the morning, there's nothing left in the evening
My dish of grass and cigarette butts topped with expired coupons.
Stir all I like; I never swallow it down.
All the while, my rabbit's foot runs about
from Las Cruces to West Memphis
searching for flawless luck.
The more one cries, the more one prospers . . .
O' ancestral demon, may my lamentation become verbal sorcery.

Hillbilly Leviathan

The Ozarks are where defeated assassins, the unholy,
and monsters come to retire.
The proper soil and crooked moonlight grows back the disemboweled,
    the decapitated,
while we collect arrears in child support for our demi-god children.

The procession of back-tail lights lined deep down the logging trails,
Along the way, there was a gentleman arguing with his soul over
    his suicide.

I, tongue of snakes.
cut up, dipped in powdered sugar,
scattered to the ants in the deepest corner of Mt. Nebo
as an insult, and bind my ghost to the mountain.

Typhoon collected the few precious scales left of me from the undertow.
My Southern accent-muscle burned up from haunting your life/house.

Now, let daybreak be my head and the year, my whole body.
An online Southern Christian university ordained my smoker's cough
to be a dove.
My favorite exorcism:
The demon, steeped in cornbread philosophy,
does not have enough ass to carry off the jeans he advertises
as he kneels down to the priest and holy water.

Years ago, as a child, I climbed the levee and made a hole in the air.
That's where I will rest, but the gate is not wide enough.
Like my burial site, I am party-sized.

CRAIG SANTOS PEREZ

Craig Santos Perez is a native Chamoru from the Pacific Island of Guåhan (Guam). He is the editor of two literature anthologies and author of three collections of poetry, most recently *from unincorporated territory [guma']* (2014), which received the American Book Award. He teaches Pacific literature and creative writing in the English Department at the University of Hawaiʻi, Manoa.

Perez's first poetry collection is *from unincorporated territory [hacha]* (2008, republished 2017), and he has since published *from unincorporated territory [saina]* (2010), and *from unincorporated territory [guma']* (2014).

from *Lisiensan Ga'lago*

"goaam" ~

    "goam" ~

"islas de las velas latinas"   (of lateen sails ~

  "guan"   "guana" ~

      "islas de los ladrones"   (of the thieves ~

"guåhan"   "guajan" ~

"islas marianas"

         (after the spanish queen ~

"bahan"   "guhan" ~

   "guacan"   "isla de san juan" ~

"guaon"

   "y guan"

"omiya jima"   (great shrine island

   "guam"

    "the first province

      of the great ocean" ~

geographic absence ~

"the old census records show"

because who can stand on the   reef
and name that below water   and sky

imagined territory ~

"a spanish baptismal name and"

burnt villages

archipelago of

"chamoru last names drawn from
the lexicon of everyday language"

bone
carved word

~

"it is possible they changed
their last names throughout their lives"

remade : sovereign

from *The Legends of Juan Malo* [a Malologue]

> ... *maps emerging out of the Pacific, maps brought in and imposed,*
> *maps combining the two, maps which are deliberate erasures and*
> *replacements; maps which reveal the rivers, mountains and geography*
> *of a people's agaga/psyche; maps used to perpetuate fictions/myths*
> *about ourselves; new maps, new fusions and interweavings* ...
> —Albert Wendt *from* "Pacific Maps and Fiction(s):
> A Personal Journey" (1991)

~

Guam is "Where America's Day Begins." Guam is the "westernmost furthest forward sovereign US territory in the Pacific." Guam is a non-self-governing colony. Guam is a US citizen ever since the 1950 Organic Act. Guam is part of the US Postal System (GU, 96910-96932). Guam "reps" the "671." Guam is a duty-free port outside the US Customs Zone. Guam is expected to homeport the Pacific feet. Guam is an acronym for "Give Us American Military." Guam is a pivot point in a realignment of US forces in the Pacific. Guam is a target. Guam is America's front porch to Asia. Guam is a mini Hawai'i. Guam is strategically invisible. Guam is published by the Guam Hotel & Restaurant Association and the Guam Visitors Bureau. Guam is a beach for sunburnt tourists in bikinis. Guam is an acronym for "Give Us Asian Money." Guam is air-conditioned. Guam is updating its Facebook status. Guam is a punch line in Hollywood movie jokes. Guam is being used to film three Hollywood Movies in the coming years. Guam is learning English as a Colonial Language (ECL). Guam is frequent flyer miles. Guam is endangered. Guam is one of [our] most curious possessions. Guam is no longer "Guam."

Ginen *the Micronesian Kingfisher* [I Sihek]

~

[our] nightmare : no
birdsong—
the jungle was riven emptied
of *[i sihek]* bright blue green turquoise red gold
feathers—everywhere : brown
tree snakes avian
silence—

the snakes entered
without words when [we] saw them it was too late—
they were at [our] doors sliding along
the passages of *[i sihek]*
empire—then

the zookeepers came—
called it *species survival plan*—captured *[i sihek]* and transferred
the last
twenty-nine micronesian kingfishers
to zoos for captive breeding *[1988]*—they repeated *[i sihek]*
and repeated :

"if it weren't for us
your birds   *[i sihek]*
would be gone
forever"

what does not change /

last wild seen—

Ginen *Tidelands* [Latte Stone Park] [Hagåtña, Guåhan]

[FOR MY DAD]

The fallen Latte *is the sign. It is from within the row of* Latte *that we feel strength. It is the severed capstone that gives us Their message, "*Ti monhayon I che'cho.*" We will not rest until the* Latte *is whole.*
—Cecilia C. T. Perez *from* "Signs of Being: A Chamoru Spiritual Journey" (1997)

~

I haligi
a pillar

i tasa
a capstone

i tataotao
a body

~

his hands—
husk coconut—

cooks and
feeds [us]—

stories—*this
raised house*—

~

at quarry
outline forms

to sing
forward—carve

limestone *to*
sing past—

~

citizen : drafted
vietnam war—

the rifle
he kept—

his uniform
his fatigue

~

soak coconut
fibers—dry

under sun—
"make rope"

braided hair—
"like this"

~

hålla haligi—
pull sky—

hålla tasa—
"pull, son"

with [our]
entire breath

~

[our] bones :
acho' latte

removed from—
to museum

of trespass—
to here—

(First Trimester)

~

[we] are watching a documentary about home
birth when [you] first feel [neni] kick // embryo

of hope // they say plastic is the perfect creation
because it never dies // litters the beaches

of oʻahu, this "gathering place" // the doctor
recommends a c-section // in the sea, plastic multiplies

into smaller pieces, leaches estrogenic and toxic
chemicals // if [we] cut open the bellies of whales

and large fish, what fragments will [we] find, derived
from oil, absorbed into tissue // because plastic

never dissolves, every product ever made still exists,
somewhere, today // i wish my daughter was made

of plastic so that she will survive [our] wasteful
hands // so that she, too, will have a great future

(Papa and Wākea)

~

earth mother and sky father
meet atop mauna kea //
hāloa naka is born
still, buried,
then sprouts // in our garden,
[we] plant nine huli
from *ku maoli ola nursery* //
'oha curves
towards the sky
like [neni's] spine
in utero // how will [we]
explain to her why
those building the largest telescope
on earth atop this mountain
yearn to see 13 billion light years
into space, yet they can't even see
the sacredness of this place
#TMTshutdown //
"look," [you] say, a raindrop
has gathered in the center
of the heart-shaped leaf
// because even [our] eyes
are 95% water

(I Tinituhon)

~

fu	ll	br	ea	th	in	gm	oo
nw	he	re	do	is	la	nd	sb
eg	in	sp	ir	al	ti	me	wa
ve	co	nt	ra	ct	io	ns	ar
ri	va	l3	0m	in	ut	es	ap
ar	t"	ha	ch	a"	th	ea	lp
ha	be	t,	ac	on	st	el	la
ti	on	of	bo	ne	ho	ok	so
ri	gi	n"	hu	ng	ga	n"	so
un	dm	ea	su	re	sa	mn	io
ti	cf	lu	id	is	90	%w	at
er	sh	ou	ld	[w	e]	go	to
th	eh	os	pi	ta	l		

166   Craig Santos Perez

GORDON HENRY, JR.

Gordon Henry, Jr. is Anishinaabe and an enrolled member of the White Earth Chippewa Tribe of Minnesota. He has earned a PhD from the University of North Dakota. His novel, *The Light People*, is winner of an American Book Award from the Before Columbus Foundation. Henry's honors include a Fulbright Lectureship in Spain. Henry serves as editor of the American Indian Studies series from Michigan State University Press.

The Failure of Certain Charms (2008) is Gordon Henry, Jr.'s first full-length poetry collection.

Simple Four Part Directions for Making Indian Lit

Ah-Beshig for the money:
Take something Indin
and take something
non
Indin
Make the Indin
indigenous or native
or skin

Make the
non
Indin
non
indigenous or
non
native
or non
skin
or white

Ah-Two: for the shonyaa
make the Indin non Indin
and the non Indin Indin
or the white Indin

Ah-T(h)ree:
Make a character out of paper
write a name with fire
or sky, or a combination of
color and the names of birds
or the absence of an article
with a present tense verb

from a limited number of infinitives
(you may) include prepositions,

except: forego, between, beyond, under
over, into, across, beside, beneath;
avoid abstractions, slang, economic terms,
hip phrases, or contemporary
situations or signs.

(You cannot use, for example, the names

> *Foregoes Hawk*
> *Under Crow*
> *Into Deer*
> *Volues Dog*
> *or Love Crane*
> *or Dances Similar*
> *or In the Middle of Night*
> *Red Thunder Bangtng*
> *or*
> *Across Wolf*
> *Eating Horse*
> *Bling Eagle*
> *or Has in Trust*
> *or Many Shoes*
> *or Sun Dude*
> *or Chick Lit*
> *or Donut Shop*
> *Yard Sale Man*
> *Beneath the Ground*
> *Upside the Head*
> *Do not Cross*
> *or Out of Position*

or Big Credit
or Bear Pimp
or Stone Suitcase
or Ice Cream Turtle
or Calls the Taxi
or Waits for Bus
or Bums a Smoke
or Speaks the Bible
Running Mascara
or Saint Muskrat
or Grafitti Clouds
or Air Flute
or Telescope Woman
or Medicine Cheese
or Karma Bull
or Missus Layups
or Nice One
or Red Exit
or Off Limits
Or even
Working Man)

So, maybe take a break
offer prayers to the polytheistic
Indo European Spirits
of syntax.

Inscribe a smoke or a ceremony

Add laughter to fighting
tears to anything
sounding like history;
reinscribe Indian

Non Indian
White.

Repeat Smoke Smudge Rinse Repeat

Imperialism
        conquest
Imperialism disease medicine
        conquest alcohol
Imperialism guns bow
        conquest
Imperialism

Make language of crossing tongues
as simple as pow wow for profit
and dying chevy hey yaw
as complex as Aristotle remains ethical
and remains remain catalogued.
Use newspapers, magazines, museum brochures,
skatagon, flint and match;
roll characters, names, words, onto paper
paper into rolls
rub with bear grease and lard,
or last night's ground beef leavings
(this will not work with
olive or sunflower oil.)
Say four hail marys, a couple of
Aho's or ah ah kaweekin
Ignite all of the above

Ah-Forza:
After all this becomes lit.
Be careful about who you
read to:

They may be hearing
Indin in everything
non Indin

(As what remains from fire is not spirit)

How Soon

The story goes from in a rainfall
to sister walking a field
browned autumn. And when she arrives
winter has come, so the old man
rises from his chair, picks up
matches, pipes and tools, and
walks out to begin again.

The sculptures grow by the day,
birds in ice, recognizable
eagles, a bear who began
as a man in a moment of dance.
He does this in ice, all
winter carving at dawn,
carving at dusk.

And sister after walking a field
browned autumn, arrives, watches
from the east window, waits,
goes out to him in spring,
taps him on the shoulder
and points to the pools
of water he's standing over.

Dear Sonny:

These lines are too much like the world we spoke of: like stoned out bragging in basements, in the rhetorical fissures of decorated walls, the whether or nots , just blowing about, talking war, world, third, first second, the prospects of discovery, the projections of the cold inner theatre, that one that talks to you before the red velvet curtain, that one that speaks before the windows prop, blinds, slatternly shadow, sun, shadow, sun, beside the wall of photographs, momentary masks you wore to wear time down to a final aperture, the sleeping field, winter, tracks of animals, over flowers and snow covered stone, little faded flags blowing about on sticks.

Shall I tell you my story, the one of grief, the one of deception, the one of travel, the one of the talk over a wooden table after a funeral, the one of the glass draining rum into a face just beyond reach in the dark? Should I tell you the story of the one I wanted to shoot, the one I wanted to love, the white feather falling from the sky, the search on the other side of the river for the lost child, the Uncle who wanted to kill your mother, the North Dakota prayers ties, on the tree we gave tea to, before we cut it. Shall I tell you the one about the ugly fights over missing articles, ownership of clothes and cars and the heart attack regalia your father wore, at the grand entry where he died? Shall I tell of the one, following the old man to a yellow house in winter where he ate with other women and woke up one Sunday to find you sleeping in a snowed over driveway, as he made his way to mass. Shall I tell you the one about the altar boy latin I could not memorize, not the words you've seen like e pluribus unum, or semper fi, or vedi, vici veni, but a whole fucking confeitor, the complete god damned lords prayer, all the litanies, the hymns, the gospels, the Friday rules. Shall I tell that one?

Every one is great here. We've burned all the firewood you cut last year. Your sister gave me your rifle. I've looked down the scope a few times and saw people walking down the road, a dog pissing on a tree, a yellow sign with holes in it, already shot at, a shirt on a line, like the one you used to wear when you went out with that Leech Lake woman, a boy across the road shooting hoops, the red galaxy you got from the old man, turned over in the yard, a cross still hanging from the rear view mirror inside, I looked hard down the scope, there was nothing worth shooting at.

Days are still numbers here, this one if I remember correctly, is a long one, day not number, just after Christmas, the 27th, no the 28th. I have to go now, the door just blew open, I hear a phone, the coffee's done, there are no words left for this day, I'm leaving like I always do, when silence and time get too deep, I go back among these people you too wanted so badly to love.

Among the Almost Decolonized

You remain one of ten
Brothers of weapons lost

In a land devoured by myths
Of strangers devoted

To regimes of pulverized
Matter fed to abused
Animals fed to men

And women who survive
With ether blasts of particles
Of a remembered better

All tethered to Stone lions
Guarding the entries
To libraries and museums

We must return to
To find ourselves
After long stretches

In enslavement

True sunrise
Comes over the
The backs of relatives

Cloud elders, the first
Bringer of light running
Morning behind them
Hill people, river people,

ridden
With dreams and
Vague recollections
Of songs for taking
Water into copper

Bowls and containers
Cut from between
The eyes of trees

Petitioned for
forgiveness

As with a language spoken
Only once a day for
Millennia of relations

We now ask
In another language
For the location
Of our weapons,
Our relatives,
With the very
Words keeping
Us bound
Floating just out of
The reach of
Those very places

The Mute Scribe Recalls Some Talking Circle

Unsettled by lies and coated with dust, a few lost species have returned
To the fire to speak of lives outside the cast of time and flow of image
invested in our own sense of the visible. Though we stand in mute as-
tonishment their language reaches us in hints and implications, trans-
lated, at times in light bands, or shifts of cold and warm, often by wind,
as when a few smaller whirling leaves circle, caught in conversations of
seasonal turn. This tells us something bigger approaches, not quite tor-
nadic, a wider swath of cyclonic energy, we feel this in our heads as an
intense pressure pushing outward as if to let out the false face dancers
we've restrained in friezes of denial and the exotic comforts of technologi-
cal asylum in squares and plazas, pixels and projections of hungry looking
women and men who have feasted on every imaginable plate of planetary
gift and resource.

The lost bird reminds us of migration, pathways of water seen from the air
as guide, a magnetic compass of some sort, as best as we can understand
in their attempts to explain flight, journey impulse and sign. The dead
flower relates, regeneration, regulation and aspiration connected to helio
force of growth nurtured in earth-spread subterranean darkness, but light
seeking, carbon breathing, air exhaling, drawn from earth, from a earlier
astro genesis of remagnetization in a long ago, forgotten place, renamed
now, again within the limits of what we understand more as mark and
sign than as vibration and heat.

The golden jackal wields another story, like a torch gesturing face to face,
as words flow in some pyronic allegory, to threaten and chase the still
beating heart back into a darkness of fear, some caved encryption of walls
signed by image older than the narrative passages of human talk.

The woman from the glittering place stories draws air rings unleashes a
story liberating clouds from gambler cachets. She sings herself away in a
few moment of thickening smoke, almost the reverse of how she said all of
her people came here.

At the end of the day all this deliberation leads to starlight, fireflies, whis-
pers and shadows, a husband barking at wife, a wife screaming, one of

the marrying speakers carrying original instructions, enters a four door vehicle and leaves, no goodbye, no language to acknowledge a final exit from this wisdom circle. He just took all his instructions, those old ways and left town in a dark buick.

BRANDY NĀLANI McDOUGALL

Brandy Nālani McDougall is of Hawaiian, Chinese, and Scottish descent from the island of Maui. She uses both English and Hawaiian language in her poetry. McDougall has earned an MFA from the University of Oregon and a PhD from the University of Hawai'i at Mānoa. McDougall is the author of the scholarly monograph *Finding Meaning: Kaona and Contemporary Hawaiian Literature* (2016).

    The Salt Wind: Ka Makani Paakai (2008) is McDougall's first book of poetry.

The Petroglyphs at Olowalu

The highway to Lāhaina, newly paved
and lined in paint, curves against the mountain,

its ridges, cutting black against the gray.
Draped in dry grass, windward slopes descend

from a cloudless sky toward Olowalu,
whose pali is sharp, abrupt. Here, the waves

carve tunnels, caves. They've outlived the hands who
pressed the lines of ghosts into the cliff-face:

stiff triangular figures, broad-shouldered
men and women, the ancestors who climb

or fall against the pali wall, buffered
by ocean wind, the salt spun fine by time.

Tracing the lines those before me began—
their words I ask for, the old work of hands.

On Cooking Captain Cook

If you ask the blonde-haired concierge
at the Grand Kīhei, he will tell you
that we ate him whole,
> strung his white meat on a stick,
> filled his mouth with apples,
> and slow-roasted him over fire.

The sunburned vendor selling t-shirts
in Lāhaina will say we ate him, too,
but only certain parts:
> the head, heart, hands
> wrapped in a kind of spinach
> and held over hot lava.

The owner of the Hoola-Hoola Bar
and Grill will say we only ate him
for lack of fine cuisine,
> rubbed his skin with sea salt
> then boiled him in coconut milk
> and served him on a bed of yams.

My anthropology professor, long researching
ancient cultures, will offer explanations
from his latest book:
> The white-skinned men seemed gods
> to those without metal or written words.
> By eating him they meant to become him.

But if you ask my tūtū
while she waters her orchids and protea
she will invite you in
to eat, to eat.

Pele‘aihonua

The curl of dawn
meets the leaving night,
lighting the black blanket
oi newborn rock, the striations
of red and rainbowed blue
that tātau your skin.
I bring this lei to ask
if I may tread here, to walk
in your house, to ask
for forgiveness. It is not enough,
this circle of lehua and tī
threaded with pule.

Your na‘au is churning
in its self-made encasement—
fire-writhing blood
of wahine, ipo, koa, akua—
Pele‘aihonua waiting.

Just yesterday I saw a man
stand by an open crevice,
use his hiking stick
to violate you, as if he could
stir your fire and
I thought, if I just pushed him,
slightly, no one would notice.

But he is not the first,
and he is one of many.

I, too, have known
the impulse to destroy,
to obliterate everything
into nothing, my na‘au
churning, waiting.

I am not the first—
I, too, am one of many

And as the fires you light
up and down the mountain
remind us, we can harden ourselves
against the salt-pricked wind.

Akā, inā kulaʻi wau, e hukiʻoe, e kuʻu akua ē?

Papatuanuku

E hoʻolohe ʻoukou e nā mamo o Hāloa—

Remember who you came from,
the first hā I gave you, binding you
to me. It is my blood coursing
through you, the lush fruit of my body
feeding you, my ʻili stretched beneath
you, its redness from which you
were formed, and my voice you hear
as your children call for you in the night,
hungry and tired with nowhere to go.

Go to them now. Hear them and hear me:

Flags hoisted, may be lowered,
spears thrown, cannons, guns,
and nuclear bombs fired, treaties
and constitutions, palapala bound
and broken. Nations rise and fall
with the tides, and your boundaries
of pepa might as well be written
in dust, for empires burn to ashes
in a fire of their own making
and will only be forgotten in the end,
when only I will remain. And through me,
so will you. He ʻoia mau no kākou.

This Island on Which I Love You

And when, on this island on which
I love you, there is only so much land
to drive on, a few hours to encircle
in entirety, and the best of our lands
are touristed, the beaches foam-laced
with rainbowing suntan oil,
the mountains tattooed with asphalt,
pocked by telescoped domes,
hotels and luxury condos blighting
the line between ocean and sky,

I find you between the lines
of such hard edges, sitting on
the kamyo stool, a bowl of coconut,
freshly grated, at your feet.

That I hear the covert jackaling
of helicopters and jets overhead
all night through our open jalousies,
that my throat burns from the scorch
of the grenaded graves of my ancestors,
the vog that smears the Koʻolaus into a blur
of greens, that I wake to hear the grind
of you blending vegetables and fruit,
machine whirl-crunching coffee beans,
your shoulder blades channelling
ocean, a steady flux of current.

Past the guarded military testing grounds,
amphibious assault vehicles emerging
from the waves, beyond the tangles
of tarp cities lining the roads, past
the thick memory of molasses coating
the most intimate coral crevices,
by the box jellyfish congregating under

'Ole Pau and Kāloa moons, at the park
beneath the emptied trees, I come
to find you shaking five-dollar coconuts
(because this is all we have on this island),
listening to the water to guess
its sweetness and youth.

On this island on which I love you,
something of you is in the rain rippling
through the wind that makes the pipes
of Waikīkī burst open, long brown
fingers of sewage stretch out
from the canal, and pesticided
tendrils flow from every ridge
out to sea, and so we stay inside
to bicker over how a plumeria tree
moves in the wind, let our daughter
ink lines like coarse rootlets
in our notebooks, crayon lines
into ladders on our walls
and sheets. Her first sentences
are sung, a moonlit blowhole plume
of sound that calls pebbles to couple,
caverns to be carved, 'uala to roll
down the hillside again, and I could
choke on this gratitude for you both.

This island is alive with love,
its storms, the cough of alchemy
expelling every parasitic thing,
teaching me to love you with
the intricacies of island knowing,
to depend on the archipelagic
spelling of you lying next to me,
our blue-screen flares their own

floating islands after our daughter
has finally fallen asleep,
to trust in the shape and curve
of your hand reaching out to hold mine
making and remaking an island our own.

Genesis

In this version of Genesis, life begins
with destruction. A sun-size star
runs out, becomes unstable, expels
a cinder seemingly lost
in the interstellar gloom.

The whole story is
in the fine grains of dust there,
still merging to form. Their ice
weaves the enormous stretches
between the stars, so that,
in the void, a giant universe

underlying all molecules
could have begun in the far
reaches of space, long before
a drifting thought of you
rolled itself up into solid
conviction. Science is hard:

It writes this story of love,
quantified in pulse and breathing,
muscle contractions, measured
in involuntary responses.

It leaves a blurred image of our
origins, the way love was meant
to be imprinted in our genes,
knotted with ending
and beginning again.

M. L. SMOKER

M. L. Smoker belongs to Assiniboine and Sioux tribes of the Fort Peck Reservation in northeastern Montana. Smoker holds an MFA from the University of Montana in Missoula where she was awarded a Richard Hugo Memorial Scholarship. She coedited *I Go to the Ruined Place: Contemporary Poems in Defense of Global Human Rights* (2009). Smoker is the director of Indian Education at the Montana Office of Public Instruction. She received a regional Emmy award for her work on the PBS documentary *Indian Relay*.

Another Attempt at Rescue is M. L. Smoker's first book of poems, published in 2005.

Casualties

"... linguistic diversity also forms a system necessary
to our survival as human beings."
—Michael Krauss

The sun has broken through.
Breaking through,
this sun—but still
today my words   are dying out.

Still as I tell of   stillness
of a very word
as (   )   as it leaves this world.

*My grandmother was told that the only way to survive was
to forget.*

Where   were you?
    Where were
you? Speaking of myself,
for   my own neglect: too often
I was nowhere to be found.
    I will not lie.
I heard the ruin in each Assiniboine voice.
I ignored them
all. On

    the vanishing, I have been
mute. I have risked
a great deal.
Hold   me   accountable

because I have not done my part
    to stay alive.

As a child I did not hear the words often enough to recognize
what I was losing.
      There are a great many parts of my own
body that are gone:

where hands
belong there is   one lost syllable.
And how a tooth might sound—
its absence
      a falling.

Sound   is so frail a thing.

(   )   hold me responsible,
in light   of failure
      I have let go   of one too many.

I have never known where or how
     to begin.

Crosscurrent

FOR JAMES WELCH

The first harvest of wheat in flatlands
along the Milk startled me into thoughts of you
and this place we both remember and also forget as home.
Maybe it was the familiarity or maybe it was my own
need to ask if you have ever regretted leaving.
What bends, what gives?
And have you ever missed this wind?—it has now
grown warm with late summer, but soon
it will be as dangerous as the bobcat stalking calves
and pets just south of the river.
Men take out their dogs, a case of beer and wait
in their pickups for dawn, for a chance with their rifles.
They don't understand that she isn't going to make
any mistakes. With winter my need for an answer
grows more desperate and there are only four roads out.
One is the same the cat hunters drive with mannish glory
and return along, gun still oil-shined and unshot.
Another goes deeper into Assiniboine territory:
This is the one I should talk myself into taking next.
I haven't much traveled the third except to visit
a hospital where, after the first time,
my mother had refused chemotherapy.
And the last road you know as well as I do—
past the coral-painted Catholic church, its doors
long ago sealed shut to the mouth of Mission Canyon,
then south just a ways, to where the Rockies cut open
and forgive. There you and I are on the ascent.
After that, the arrival is what matters most.

Equilibrium

IN MEMORY OF ERIC LEVI BIGLEGGINS

I

After child after child after child, no one
believes in the cacophony of sirens anymore.

If only we could break back these bones
and form a new ceremony from each of our losses.

O' mend our teeth from another dark stretch of road,
our rugged knuckles from another first of the month.

2

And still the children keep jumping from trains.
The people in town dream anxiously,
fire and iron licking at the corners of old,
handmade quilts. They have forgotten
the language of antelope and creek bed,
find in its place only one way to say
we are not responsible.

Today one man woke to the callous offering
of a bird's beak and black wing
left on his doorstep at daybreak.
And what of all the other warnings,
of all the family lost because their hearts
were too heavy for them to carry?
If we could put these omens away, down in the basement
the door could be locked,
the mutter of crows left there to decay.

3

Next time and it will be the dance of chairs
and imaginary high speed chases.
It will require a fine sense of balance
and a song of stars.
Just the slightest slip of the rope
and the sky will be set
loose, the body
like a shift in the river's current.

4

The Bridge can hold, the body can not, and our excuses
will do nothing to save us now.

We survive between these barbed wire
fabrications. We gather together in the middle of the night,
call out the names of lost cousins and friends who cannot
cross over to the other side because we keep
praying them back.
We ask so much of them: *slow the car down, don't jump,
don't let go, come back to us.*

But what are we really guilty of?—the blood memory of what
we can't forgive ourselves for.

5

Hollowed out grief becomes electric,
loosens a thousand storm patterns
in the marrow of ghost homes,
ghost children, ghost love.

We are the ones

FOR DEZMOND

Waiting.

A syllable: forming,

generating energy in small, dark masses: marrow, stem cell, neuron.

Waiting to come alive again in this tiny body.

Guwa—you should learn this is the word between you and I,

my son, *hokshina*.

    Come here. Come home. To this place. Between you and I

no separation. But always room. And silence—until

we can find meaning and the words together.

I repeat it, again and again, gesturing for you to come over. Hoping

the vibrations will come alive, you will listen inside yourself. And you
  will sense

just who you are, who you belong to and among.

As if you were under water and could feel your pulse,

the whir and swish of your blood traveling miles and miles.

  Across the wind-blown graves of your great grandparents and
    their grandparents—

Mikushi, Mitugash—yours. And they are out there, belonging to you
  before

you were even born. Waiting.

Heart Butte, Montana

The unsympathetic wind, how she has evaded me for years now,
leaving a guileless shell and no way to navigate. Once when I stood
on a plateau of earth just at the moment before the dangerous,
jutting peaks converged upon the lilting sway of grasslands, I almost
found a way back. There, the sky, quite possibly all the elements,
caused the rock and soil and vegetation to congregate. Their prayer
was not new and so faint I could hardly discern. Simple remembrances,
like a tiny, syncopated chorus calling everyone home: across
a thousand eastward miles, and what little wind was left at my back.
But I could not move. And then the music was gone.
All that was left were the spring time faces of mountains, gazing down,
their last patches of snow, luminous. I dreamed of becoming snow melt,
gliding down the slope and in to the valley. With the promise,
an assurance, that there is always a way to become bird, tree, water again.

LEANNE HOWE

LeAnne Howe is an enrolled member of the Choctaw Nation of Oklahoma. Her novel *Shell Shaker* is a Before Columbus Foundation American Book Award winner. She is coeditor of *Seeing Red, Pixeled Skins: American Indians and Film 2013.* Her memoir *Choctalking on Other Realities* is winner of the 2014 MLA Prize for Studies in Native American Literatures, Cultures, and Languages. Howe holds the Eidson Distinguished Professorship in the Department of English at the University of Georgia, Athens.

Evidence of Red is LeAnne Howe's first collection of poems, published in 2005. Her second book is *Savage Conversations* (2019).

A Duck's Tune

Ya kut unta pishno ma*
Ya kut unta pishno ma
Ya kut unta pishno ma
Ya kut unta pishno ma

So I moved to this place,
Iowa City, Ioway
Where green-headed mallards
walk the streets day and night,
and defecate on sidewalks.
Greasy meat bags in wetsuits,
disguise themselves as pets
and are as free as birds.
Maybe Indians should have thought of that?

Ya kut unta pishno ma
Ya kut unta pishno ma
Ya kut unta pishno ma
Ya kut unta pishno ma

Maybe you would have
left us alone,
if we put on rubber bills,
and rubber feet,
Quacked instead of complained,
Swam instead of danced
waddled away when you did
what you did . . .

Ya kut unta pishno ma
Ya kut unta pishno ma
Ya kut unta pishno ma
Ya kut unta pishno ma

---

* This is a dance refrain for a song. The phrase is to be performed. Ya kut unta
pishno ma means *"We were doing this." Dancing.*

So I moved to the Place
The "Jewel of the Midwest"
Where ghosts of ourselves
Dance the sulphur trails.

Fumes emerge continuous
from the mouths of
Three-faced Deities who preach,
"We absolve joy through suffering."

Ya kut unta pishno ma
Ya kut unta pishno ma
Ya kut unta pishno ma
Ya kut unta pishno ma

So I moved to this place where
in 1992, up washed Columbus again
like a pointy-chinned Son of Cannibals.
His spin doctors rewrite his successes
"After 500 years and 25 million dead,
One out of 100 American Indians commit suicide
One out of 10 American Indians are alcoholics
49 years is the average lifespan of American Indians."

Each minute burns
the useful and useless alike
Sing Hallelujah
Praise the Lord

Ya kut unta pishno ma
Ya kut unta pishno ma
Ya kut unta pishno ma
Ya kut unta pishno ma

And when you foreigners
build your off-world colonies
and relocate in outer space
This is what we will do
We will dance,
We will dance,
We will dance
to a duck's tune.

Ya kut unta pishno ma
Ya kut unta pishno ma
Ya kut unta pishno ma
Ya kut unta pishno ma

Finders Keepers: Aboriginal Responses to European Colonization

Almost three hundred years ago
Mississippi Choctaw women took
Frenchmen into their beds
into their *iksas,*
into their hearts
for their blood.
The men called this ritual
the sweet medicine of immortality.

Bread is the human body
Bread confers immortality.
When my story is finished,
You will offer yourself again to me like bread.
Unafraid.
And I will take you.
My God you are brave.
Have you forgotten what Grandmother said?

That the women of my family
are like the plants
we call *bashuchak.*
Everlastings

Ballast

Dear Dean,

I know what you mean. Like shipping costs from China, all things rise over Okieland, bodies, baseballs, Wiley Post's eye, *you remember that eye*, my adopted father's right arm as he pitches a ball so high into the great blue yonder, I lost sight of it in 1958.

If we were home, (and we're not) I would show you Wiley Post Airport one block from the house on Hatley Street in Bethany, Oklahoma where I was raised along with a yard of chickens and images of Wiley Post in his pressure suit hovering above us. Sometimes his sub-stratospheric flights without enough O_2 make his good eye go gaga like the ones we saw in Modigliani paintings, *you remember those eyes*. Raised up in Maysville, Wiley was quintessential Okie, an ex-con turned oil field roughneck turned parachute jumper turned aviation inventor. He and the Cherokee kid Will Rogers were up 26,000 feet when their plane engine failed. No screaming, no sorrow, no hubris, just three lines over Alaska.

Point Barrow
26 thousand feet, we're in a vertical dive.
Orion-Explorer seaplane in . . .

If we were there, (and we weren't) I would have elbowed,

Oklahoma here we come!

Catafalque
June 1875
Bellevue Place Sanitarium 333 Jefferson Street, Batavia, Illinois

Midnight, Mary Todd Lincoln's bedroom. The underarms of her nightdress are badly soiled. Her small feet are swollen; the skin is paper-thin.

Savage Indian has a small box on his lap filled with her jewelry. He fingers each piece and finally fastens a pearl necklace around his neck.

Mary Todd Lincoln
Nightly I examine the ruined heads in my handheld mirror: yours and mine, our eyes dangle like dull grapes on a broken vine, is it the candlelight?

Savage Indian *Watches her with menacing eyes but does not move.*

Mary Todd Lincoln
I touch the blemish on your face, finger your blood-stained shirt, a drop of spittle has escaped your tight lips, your bare feet clammy as fish, all there, and here; I kiss the mirror, beg you to wake, fight to catch your attention through some mad, theatrical gesture, remember? My bed, always a catafalque to you; Oh let fly my flesh, hair, and eyelash, pay the Nightjar who regularly serenades, but like us, steals the milk of goats.

Here, at last, I'll tell it all; I did wish you dead, Sir, eight thousand thirty-nine times for all the days you ran sideways from our home, whistling a Nightjar's tune. Pay them all now Sir, before dawn's light.

Savage Indian *Reads aloud the inscription of her wedding ring.*
Love is Eternal.

Catafalque II
June 1875
Bellevue Place Sanitarium 333 S. Jefferson Street, Batavia, Illinois

Mary Todd Lincoln and Savage Indian pace around the room like amateur boxers.

Mary Todd Lincoln
Arriving nightly without invitation,
You make my room a ceremony as
Nightjars sing, wing clap, chirr a bird's song.
Inhibited at dawn by God's will, like us.

When shall I tell them the truth?
Where shall I keep the truth?
Under my frayed petticoat,
It will not flower now.

She fingers a small picture of Abraham Lincoln on her bureau.

There is no need to wait for tea: I confess
I did long for the pleasure of your coarse skin,
Money to spend, kid gloves, chiffon and satin
Ball gowns with lavish trains properly hemmed. Doomed children.

Tonight, let us hoist the catafalque over a new grave
Hold my hands above the dank earth as the Nightjars serenade
Oh what a great heart smasher you are, Mr. Lincoln.
Adieu, my confessor, my all-in-all, lover, protector, ghost husband.

Turning to Savage Indian.

Wishing for nothing, not even breath,
Take the flint knife,
Cut me, I dare you.

The Rope[1] Seethes

Out of Fort Snelling's coffin
I swing like a fool on holiday
Backward, forward, and
Around and around

---

[1] A single noose from the December 26, 1862, Dakota hangings has been preserved in the collections of Fort Snelling, Minnesota. In 2011 representatives from the Dakota Nation visited the collection to see the noose. Prayers were offered. For additional readings see *The Thirteenth Turn: A History of the Noose,* by Jack Shuler.

CEDAR SIGO

Cedar Sigo was raised on the Suquamish Reservation in the Pacific Northwest and studied at the Jack Kerouac School of Disembodied Poetics at the Naropa Institute. Sigo is the editor of *There You Are: Interviews, Journals, and Ephemera,* on Joanne Kyger. Sigo lives in San Francisco and is editor of Old Gold Press.

Selected Writings is Cedar Sigo's first collection of poems, published in 2003 and revised and expanded for a 2005 publication. Sigo is also author of eight books, including *Expensive Magic* (2008), *Stranger in Town* (2010), *Language Arts* (2014), and *Royals* (2017).

Now I'm a Woman

When you hear the knives ring
Turn the page.
I wonder why I am not
Myself of late, ridiculous glass edges
Turn back on themselves
And soon reveal
The hand of an apprentice
And godforsaken embarrassing torch,
Stormy back hallways
Out of the black and wooden theaters.
Crystal Waters plus her driver
Plus her entourage is still rolling out
Of the sands, Atlantic City
On soundtracks to shows
Held over at The Fairmount
She is throwing back shots
With the mafia. I have learned
To take apart this American Songbook
And very fortunately as I would take
My audience in confidence
Threads of gold fall closely together
Coming to break us off.
At the first if the shows
I sang this song
And in between I saw him in the hall,
What could I tell you?
"Someday we'll build on a hilltop high."

Thrones

For Phillis Wheatley: A book of verse uncovered in cornerstones of a Moorish castle, purple and gold depicting souls in various stages of release, the pitch, anger and arc of the poems an unrhymed mirror to the long Atlantic.

For Jayne Cortez: An intertribal grand entry of poets in cedar bark jackets split skirts and whalebones pinning them closed, a voice in praise and suspension of the drum.

For Amiri Baraka: The Pisan cantos decoder ring dipped in black hills gold slipped onto the finger of Donyale Luna who is Cleopatra reborn sleeping soundly in bed.

For Bob Kaufman: A clamp for the mind, docking in a Persian house of ill repute, a striped gabardine diary and the American prison system picked open with an amethyst knife.

For Henry Dumas: A window open on the fog of New York. A studio with desk lamp and a shadow of his writing self pointing back at certain habits, taking off his coat to sit, spilling a little coffee, with all of eternity waiting enthralled.

For Bob Thompson: An all expense paid trip back to Rome on a riverboat tied with roses, its ballroom filled with golden ghouls and hugely debutant postures collapsed, the walls are wet with organ music.

For Alice Coltrane: A custom isolation booth the exact size of Stravinsky's last silhouette. He stares out. He taps from behind the green glass.

For Stephen Jonas: Your favorite Eric Dolphy faded to a room of golden tasseled light. A couch of friends' faces smeared in a gleaming silver crown

Green Rainbow Song

Hung up on
my hearing
and deep in whose
playbook
one too many
nights and never
a black-out
Doing the best
I can, only a man
it hurts me too
Blues in the Night
Verlaine Blues
sitting here thinking
a blues for Anne
(all nerves)
and mine
the most dirty
unhurried
afternoon jags
A freshly penned
lyric for sinking
to autumnal
Atlantean shade
I wish us more luck
I wish my little
tiger lily sheltered
in a clear crystal
box (being carried)
Green pearl-handled
mallets edging
the annunciation
toward a new burn
The chamber of maiden
thought is metered
Big fields

villagers, stars
on the back-lot blues
It's the smoke spot
I shade softest
a curve so tight
it's really blind
The chamber gives
way to the word
in this case (mine)

Things to Do in Suquamish

FOR JASON MORRIS

Smoke Salmon

       Call San Francisco————————————"Like . . . Totally!"

              Get driven to the terminal,
                         escape.

         Come back after dark and feed the horses:

                     alfalfa
                     timothy
                     oats

              Pick their hooves.

      Visit the Suquamish Museum

the eyes of Chief Seattle are shut (his spirit to himself)

sepia tones, baskets, white-hot rocks

        cobalt trade beads

      Say "hi" to all my cousins   (cul-de-sac)

"Hi Josh!"

"Hi Jeremyl"

                Drink Rainier beer

              a red ribbon
                  out up
              and one the peak
                        (I confuse it with Mount Fuji)

              Walk back to dad's room.
He talks when he wants and smokes, linger over his bookshelf

Moby-Dick, Starling Street, all of Kurt Vonnegut.

                  Try and write the serial killer light at night

        (see-through

                green & black)

                    Give up. Try Prose.

Taken Care Of

I come from Inuit oil money,
From instruments of chance and divination.
The most loose, shut in, wavering mind,
Recording my day with recitations, antennae,
Narration and figure, my phone might die. I'm walking dirty.
Shop and mob cops, not to touch my mother's breast
Or the queen's royal crown signature
Izzy Juju—hijacked, forsaking all others.
The untamed scotch is mine. It cost the picture a fortune
To say nothing of my turban, costume copies
Of topaz bracelets, the umpteenth translation.
Did you ever know Micah, Gay Sunshine, Grace Cathedral, Coconut?
I went from heels at Barneys to the depths of the bins.
Who could be like dropping in? I'll fold both my hands
In gloves and wait, Hope Diamond peeking out.

Aquarelle

Bent at my
desk
in pieces
in starlight's
wire clutch
the eye is caught
staring into splinters
like the warble of
the dove at the start
of rain, and the curve
of the cane
to follow its script,
the lord of
the nadir is
the black sun,
a hot whiskey
with anise wash,
small circular brush
to lash and gather
to be trans
not destroyers
continuous snowfall
recorded, crystals
tapping colors
out from their centers
my idealized
voice in fact
a ruin
I can't freeze
lines together
any longer
I need hot flowers,
figures ripped
loudly from

their boxes rather
off balance
crumbling smoke
losing the light
lifted

Light Unburied, Unchained

FOR JACK GIESEKING

I am leaving to be driven down to Mexico City
    The line between seems incidental

I am going underground in Oaxaca
    to flip through rare European monographs on air conditioned
      mezzanines
                  Odilon Redon's *Angel in Chains*, Joan Mitchell's
            blighted canary and fuchsia permissions (wings)

In the longest dreams I sail my raft to Puerto Vallarta
    Thin mauve and pink bands in the sky lie still and hold clear like the
      tropics, the equator

Brazen heatwaves slice the earth in half . . .

If Brian and I are allowed to land in San Miguel
    The young horses will sprout wings and become handsome, sought
      after devils.

I will lead a rebellion through the streets of Patzcuaro
    and lose my head which (unattached) will continue to organize and
      write
                  and reverberate! Become immortalized in oil
            a large head, wrought of light
                  painted by Leonora Carrington

Double Vision

Dry tip golden
        as sunken
                points
        of arrows (voices)
a phantom's near
                to dissolving night
        swarm
of locusts
            down iron post
    in cross
        of wind
all erasure
                of William
        Carlos Williams
stars unfold
        throughout pendants
and
    no further
                cool the tendons
        advancement
                    in splayed
        crepe myrtle
tall teetering
                voices tonight
    how many
plots
        are gained
            from a book
of his poems?
                    dumb
        fuck-heads leaving
no ruins

           a stick
       is pointed
at the empty
               corner
       a master-work (withheld)
                    claw-foot bathtub
       extra bleed

integral illusions
                        of relief
           shoulder to
shoulder gunmen
           form a cube
scene in
           nearest sky
                    thread splits
       from sharkskin
waistcoats
               back-view
                        jolted
                          off the hook
           the several
sounded out
               munitions
                        in my voice

KARENNE WOOD

Karenne Wood is a member of the Monacan Indian tribe. She has served on the National Congress of American Indians' Repatriation Commission and has researched Native history for the National Museum of the American Indian. A linguistic anthropologist, Karenne Wood grew up in the suburbs of Washington, DC. She earned an MFA at George Mason University and held a Ford Fellowship at the University of Virginia, where she completed a PhD. Wood is the director of Virginia Indian Programs at Virginia Humanities.

Markings on Earth is Karenne Wood's first collection of poems, published in 2001. Her second collection is *Weaving the Boundary* (2016).

Amoroleck's Words

You can't take a man's words.
They are his even as the land
is taken away
where another man
builds his house.
                    —Linda Hogan

You must've been a sight, Captain John Smith
as your dugout approached
with Jamestown's men
sporting plumed hats,
poufed knickers, beards, stockings,
funny little shoes.
You might have looked, to us,
well,
uncivilized.
We fought you, we know,
because you wrote it down.
One man was left behind. Wounded.
At your mercy. Among your shining goods—
mirrors, knives, firearms, glass beads—
where was mercy? Maybe you left it
in England. Eager to learn, Captain Smith,
you asked about the worlds he knew,
whether there was gold,
why his people had fought
when you came to them "in love."
He told you in his dialect,
which no one now speaks.
You recorded his name. His words.
Not his fate.

Of all the words our people spoke
in the year of your Lord 1608,
only his answer remains:
*"We heard that you were a people
come from under the world,
to take our world from us."*

My Standard Response

I.

The first question is always phrased this way:
"So. How much Indian *are* you?"

II.

We did not live in tepees.
We did not braid our hair.
We did not fringe our shirts.
We did not wear war bonnets.
We did not chase the buffalo.
We did not carry shields.
We were never Plains Indians.
We tried to ride,
but we kept falling off of our dogs.

III.

A local official came to our office to ask our help with a city event. He had a splendid idea, he said. To kick off the event and show everyone in town that our tribe was still around, we should go up to the bluff over-looking the city and make a big smoke signal. Then they would know we were here.

Who ever heard of smoke signals in the forests? I imagined us up on the bluff, lighting one of those firestarter bricks. We haven't made fire since the Boy Scouts took over. And how would the citizens know it was us? They'd probably call out the fire department.

IV.

As they ask, they think, *yes,*
I can see it in her face. High cheekbones
(whatever those are) *and dark hair.*

Here's a thought: don't we all have
high cheekbones? If we didn't,
our faces would cave in.

(But I do have a colonized nose.)

I'm sick of explaining myself.

"You know," I finally say,
"It doesn't matter to my people."
I ride off to my ranch-style home.
Time to weave a basket, or something.

In Memory of Shame

because it was our fault and because we did nothing wrong
because we spoke and because we had nothing to say
because we were ignorant and because we knew too much
because we neglected our children and because we wanted to
because we drank and because we stopped drinking
because we were industrious and because we had no energy
because we were young, old, fat, bony, spineless, cocky,
     selfish, selfless, frigid, immoral, guilty

     because we loved too much or not enough
     because we couldn't fry an egg correctly
     because the house hid dust in its corners
     because we stayed and because we left
     because our faces were the wrong ones
     because we were treated disrespectfully
     because we were children or women or not
          white or just not enough.

because we wanted to protect them

Abracadabra, an Abcedarian

All this time I've been looking for words for certain difficult women because they aren't able to speak for themselves, and now the Clinton Foundation has come up with a brilliant campaign—they decided for International Women's Day, through digital magic to erase women on the cover of *Condé Nast*, posters, billboards, those figures replaced by empty space because women have not yet achieved gender equity, as noted on a website, not-there.org, and they're right. We haven't. But when I read about not-there.org and saw its flashy graphics, I wasn't thinking about how women are not-there-yet, metaphorically, I just thought about women who are really not there, women and girls who keep disappearing (not from magazines, who don't make news in Manhattan) like they've evaporated, like illusions, hundreds in Juárez, twelve hundred missing and murdered Native women across Canada. The hands of men.

Now you see her. Not. Not-there. Not here, either,

or anywhere. Maybe only part of the problem is the predatory perpetrator-prestidigitator who more often than not knows her, knows how to keep her quiet, who may claim to love her, even, maybe getting even—or the serial rapist-killer in the bushes who bushwhacks her in the dark. You're always safe, says the forensic psychiatrist, unless a monster happens to show up, and then you're not. Not-there. Maybe a lonely mandible, maxilla, fibula, or ulna shows up, or a bagged body gets dragged from the river. Or not. Is this the value we permit a woman's life to have (or not-have) throughout a wrong world, a global idea of her as disposable parts? In the end, this is not a xenophobic poem, not specific—it's everywhere. Not-there. Right here. Yes, the sun rises anyway, but now the parents are staring past each other, that zero between them like a chalked outline in their family photograph. Or not.

Bartolomé de las Casas, 1542

So it was that we discovered a flowering island we named "Hispaniola"
which natives called Haití, or Mountains, and Quisqueya, Mother of Lands.

And the people were guileless, generous, devoid of wicked thought.
They coveted not. They were delicately built, suited poorly for labor.

Into this land of the meek came our Spaniards like ravening beasts,
with methods of torture never heard of before; to such a degree, I believe,

that a number of three million souls is now not exceeding two hundred,
in less than fifty years. Who will believe it? More than thirty islands,

ruined, land pocked in a mad search for gold, people thrown into slavery,
nations destroyed on the mainland; I imagine fifteen million people killed.

Indian men hid children and wives, saying Christians could not have come
from Heaven, and still our Spaniards cut them to pieces, sparing few,

with such abandon that I feared for our souls. Away from laws that govern
civil men, they became worse than brutes; the war dogs were kinder,

for they killed to eat and did not so loudly enjoy it. What of the survivors?
The men died in the mines, women died in the fields, without time

or place to come together. The milk in the women's breasts dried up, infants
perished, and thus was emptied that place which had seemed paradise.

The Poet I Wish I Was

1. A white poet whose work I admire said she feels most inspired on her daily four-mile walk through a forest.

2. I wish I had time to walk four miles daily. I can usually manage one mile with dogs. My dogs are distractible, and they distract me.

3. The Native poet I wish I was gets up early to walk dogs through a forest and comes home to her desk overlooking a lake. She spends half the day swimming with dogs, the other half reading and writing. Dogs are pleased. She is mostly inspired.

4. The poet I wish I was travels around like a famous Indian poet I know, reading and speaking and accepting awards. I don't care much about awards—I just want my poems to be better, like his. (That's a lie. Every poet wants all of the awards.)

5. The famous Native poet kept writing about his dead father. He said he's made mostly of his dad. "Like water." It's a short poem.

6. The poet I wish I was spent her childhood walking through a forest, because that's where Indians belong, right? She didn't spend her childhood wishing she could be a child whose father didn't leave, believing it was her fault, then seeking out men who would leave her.

7. I never wanted to be that famous Indian poet. I wanted to be his best friend or his older sister. The one who walked out of that drunken house fire in Montana. The sister who lived.

8. I wanted to be that poet's father. The one who didn't die of kidney failure, alcohol related. The Indian father who lived.

9. I wanted to be my own father. The one who didn't die of cirrhosis, alcohol related. The Indian father who lived. I wanted to be my own father so that he could still be alive.

10. How fucked up is that?

11. The poet I wish I was is grateful to Indian fathers who stay alive, who work hard so their kids don't go hungry. Who want to be better, like my brother, who is a good father. We all just want to be better.

12. My kids never went hungry. They ate canned corn and baloney for years.

13. Many of the poets I admire have leapt or fallen from the perches where I stuck them carefully like plastic Jesuses, again and again.

14. However good we are, we can't change the beginning or the middle— we can only try to rewrite the end.

ERIC GANSWORTH

Eric Gansworth (S·ha-weñ na-sae’) is an enrolled member of the Onondaga Nation. A multigenre writer, he is author of the novels *Mending Skins*, *Extra Indians*, and *If I Ever Get Out of Here*, a young adult novel. His honors include awards from PEN Oakland, Before Columbus Foundation, Lannan Foundation, and New York Foundation for the Arts. He is a professor of English and Lowery Writer-in-Residence at Canisius College in Buffalo, New York.

Nickel Eclipse is Eric Gansworth’s first collection of poems, published in 2000. Gansworth’s second collection is *A Half-Life of Cardio-Pulmonary Function* (2008).

Speaking through Our Nations' Teeth

When you see me
for the first time
at a powwow or social
across the circle
we dance
in which language and world view
do you form your first
impression

the one you were taught
in school, memorizing epics
and heroes of other
people, diagramming
sentences with the precision
of a surgeon, driving
modifiers and prepositional
phrases beneath the horizon
like roots or
dead relatives
or both

or the ones you were taught
hiding beneath
your mother's dining room
table, where she
and her generation
forgot you were there and
spoke of the giant turtle, the twins
the grandmother moon and said
"Jeh-oos' eh, awk-r(h)ee aw(t)-ness"
to one another, laughing
without fear of you
learning and growing
this voice they thought
would only keep you behind

I listen, for Cheweant; Skenno; She'kon;
Guuwaadze; Hensci, estonko; Boozhoo;
Dah-leh; osiyo; ready to bare these teeth
in a smile where we find ourselves
and each other.

It Goes Something Like This

I have heard this story
before, she walks alone
her moccasins cracking east
coast sand kernels
along the white-washed Atlantic
City Boardwalk waiting
for the train that will take her
to a school she'd only heard of
that morning, discovering
strangers and a packed bag
with her parents as she came down
for breakfast, and suddenly the midway
music is cut by the more familiar
sounds of home, someone
singing a Tuscarora Social song.
He is dark and she joins in the song
as they, two children, view the ocean
together for the first time.
They board the train and share
a seat the rest of the way
to Carlisle Indian School
and are married as
soon as they graduate.

Many voices have repeated
in the best oral tradition
this story of my grandparents
with great vividness
the beadwork design
in her moccasins
the song he sang
bending my doubting questions silent.
As I start to ask why
they hadn't known
each other on the reservation

or at least seen each other board
or why the New York
to Pennsylvania train stopped
at the New Jersey coastline
I realize they could have met
emptying Headmaster chamber pots
or as voices in black
isolation chambers for speaking
a language still their only link
and I am satisfied with the version
I hear. Sometimes the story is
enough to bring me home.

Repatriating Ourselves

There is no need
for you to give
back to us
what we already own

This is who we are
in the present
tense

no climate control
no tatters of cloth
no catalogued bones
no beads on loan
no boxes
no labels
no ceremonial tables
no tags
no medicine bags
no hermetic sealers
no deadly disease
no hypotheses
no educated guesses
no dioramas
no dramas
no arrays of diaspora disconnects
no displays of personal effects

in the present
tense
this is who we are

what we already own
there is no need
for you to give
back to us

Snagging the Eye from Curtis

The first time I saw you,
I noticed immediately
that your tones were brown
but not sepia
that there were no herds
of headless buffalo
dotting the landscape
behind you
no questionable blanket
mantled across your shoulders
no sun perpetually setting
on the mesas and plateaus
heaving themselves around you
in authenticity—
that you were not

> a daguerreotype
> a tintype
> a stereotype
> a bloodtype "I +"

percentages marked
by the yardstick
of a photographer
nearly convincing us
a century ago
we were ghosts trapped within
his snapping shutter

who was unaware
we could learn
where the F stopped
and how the light
metered out the ways
we knew ourselves
to be and not to be,
no question.

A Half-Life of Cardio-Pulmonary Function

I used to think
that if I loved hard
enough and long enough
passion would always win out

like the way I loved
cologne, venturing teenaged into
congested malls, abusing testers
only a salesperson surly enough

inquiring if he or she could help
me in any way, spitting
the prices of even the smallest
bottles of the scents I had

slathered on, forcing me out
in a cloud of confidence
that I was the Calvin Klein
Man, not the Old Spice

Man, not the Zest
Man, and certainly not
the My Drafty House is Warmed Badly
by Kerosene Heaters Man

impervious to my real
life where I would sneak
down in the middle
of the night, passing

snow collecting
on the inside of the window
sill, trying to descend
the stairs silently

to complete the night lying
before the stove's vents blowing
sooty warm air deep into my
sleeping lungs, clutching

a broken lacrosse stick
to intimidate rats so brazen
our housecats accepted
them as equal occupants

until I exit those automatic
doors, leave fountains where
just out of range I envy white
families tossing entire

cigarettes packs' worth
of what they call spare
change, wishing for things
they could already buy if they wanted

laughing as those presidential
faces fall sometimes up
and sometimes down, all drowning
in three inches of chlorinated well water

return to the reservation
where my sister-
in-law embraces me later
the same day, drawing

deeply, saying she loves
the scent of burned heating
oil on men, that it reminds
her of when she and my brother

dated and she would hold
him long in those last moments
before allowing him to walk out
her door, meander through snowy

grooves, finding his way home
while she looked out windows
where ice crystals gathered
on the proper side of the pane

holding her breath as long as she
dared, letting his presence seep
out only when she could no longer
bear, leaving him to be a vapor ghost

on her window, a fog sure
to vanish even before she turned
from the window and here I am
years later, living in that same

state, you miles away and I
knowing how presence disperses
into air, wonder how long
I can hold my breath.

. . . Bee

I stood in a longhouse
with a woman who may or may not
be Mohawk. Some shift their opinions
about her like meteorologists, as if
her blood were a storm system tracked
in its comings and goings. But the father
of her two sons was, without question, Seneca.
We knew that, in Haudenosaunee country, a father
is to some degree irrelevant, that her own
shifting identity would impact her sons' lives
like a gene vulnerable to betrayal, causing
certain, terminal conditions. She waited
on an elder she called Steam, (warning I was not
to call the elder woman by that name). Steam
(not Steam) would observe the boys, understand
their natures, give them their Creator names defining
their lives during the next ceremony. I confessed
my namelessness, confessed my longhouse and fluency
deficient community, and confessed that my clan
mother, three hours away, did not know me well
enough to give me a name, confessed my community followed
a more casual ceremony. You find your name after a social misstep,
a dubious facial feature, a birth defect. Names offer
the name-givers comfort, that your challenge is harder
than theirs, no matter the truth.

Our names are a convoluted toughening of our skins. My name
is not like Steam, (no one is forbidden to use it). No one
calls me Batman because of my status, my utility
belt, my impressive batpole, my agility, my muscles,
my profile in spandex, my virtues, but because I wore
the cape to an older age than I should have, and could
continue to wear it now, as that shit is not going away
anytime soon. Even kids who only know Christian Bale
or Michael Keaton, lurking in latex and leather hood,
still think Batman is my name.

And this is why I have no memory for when or how you became
the Bumblebee, what it means, beyond the literal.
You soar in gardens, spend days ensuring growth,
and if metaphors are at work here, this one seems true
enough to keep you in amber wings, fuzzy yellow rings,
black lacquer torso, and sensitive antennae.

What metaphor suits the night I left on the Amtrak
for Chicago, past 1:00 a.m., while you stood
on the platform, watching those cars pull out,
the night I wanted to leap from the train, stay?

I cannot invent new names for the ways we slow,
struggle, attempt to maintain the illusion of futures
without measure, defy actuary numbers and because I have
gone closer to the light than you have, the story is
easier to craft and finesse, than it should be.

Pollination trails are smaller than those I'm forced
to fly in, and lying in Little Rock, Santa Fe, Manhattan,
Minneapolis, Seattle, hotel rooms, the ellipse of your name
trail winds me home, waiting, dusted in pollen and history.

JANET McADAMS

Janet McAdams is of Scottish, Irish, and Creek (Muscogee) ancestry. She won the Diane Decorah First Book Award from the Native Writers Circle of the Americas and an American Book Award in poetry. She is the author of a novel, *Red Weather*. McAdams earned her MFA in poetry from the University of Alabama and her PhD in comparative literature from Emory University. She teaches at Kenyon College as the Robert P. Hubbard Professor of Poetry. In 2005, she founded the award-winning Earthworks Poetry Series for Salt Publishing in the UK.

The Island of Lost Luggage is Janet McAdams's first collection of poems, published in 2000. Her second collection is *Feral* (2007). Her chapbook, *Seven Boxes for the Country After*, was published in 2016.

The Hands of the Taino

Laid out on vellum, the past
Is a long wound. It unfolds
Five centuries later,
Beneath the heavy pen of scholars.
The world shifts and spins
As the Admiral's bronze astrolabe
Measures the paths between stars.
The sky is written in the sea's
Uneasy mirror, and mermaids
Comb their hair in the distance.
They are not, he writes, *so beautiful*
as I have heard. He dreams of his own
circuitous route to the Heavens.
God and the Crown. Both want too much

II. GOVERNOR

At Guanahani, they swam to the caravel
Bearing parrots and balls of cotton thread,
These people so unlike him they could not
not be saved.
                Too angry to sleep,
The Governor haunts every room in his castle.
The servants whisper in their own tongue.

The severed hands of the Taino
Wave in clear salt water,
In pink-tinted water.
They wave as the gold mines dry up,
As the Governor leaves Hispaniola in chains.

Mermaids, dog-headed men and women
With breastplates of copper—

They draw their bows, and arrows
Cover the shore of Columbus's dream.
No, not the Taino, whom he once called *in dios*.
They touch his white skin.

They have the faces of Christian angels.

Leaving the Old Gods

I.

The people who watch me hang my coat
On a peg at the office don't even know
about the other life,
the life when there was you, *it*,
however briefly. To them my body
is a fact casual as the weather.
I could tell them:
That day it rained
the way it rains in the New World.
Leaves struck the window like daggers.
I didn't think about *God*
But the ones we used to worship
The ones who want your heart still
Beating, who load you with gold
and lure you to sleep
deep in the cenote.

II.

A girl, he said, and I nodded
though we couldn't have known.
I would have left him then
for ten thousand pesos.
I don't know what world you inhabit,
swimming there, baby, not-baby,
part of my body, not me,
swept aside like locks of hair
or toenail parings.
It's ten years today
and you who were never alive
pull a face in the leaves
of jacaranda, the only tree
that lives outside my window.

It must be your voice
Whistling through the office window,
Though I can't understand your words.
Comfort or accusations,
I can't understand your words.

Ghazal of Body

Teach me the story of the sleepless body.
Even the past is ugly, living as it does in the thick cells of my body.

I was lonely, all the long winter. Skin
the poorest fence between the cold world and my body.

The fisherman with his sharp hook, his taut line, a rod he is proud of.
Come to shore, I call, I have a handful of bread that might be your body.

Lace, you breathed against the window, and the ice let go,
ran down the glass into the house's quiet body.

She said: *When I gave him up, when I gave back the baby,*
there was an empty space in front of my body.

No writ, no photograph, no stone with rules. Only memory,
running like a current of blood, through the creek of my body.

from *"The Collectors"*

iii
Catalog

Open it, the bursting door:
elephant's foot,
shrunken head,
Princess Venus,
Lemon Cockle,
the Lightning Whelk,
the Hawk Wing Conch,
stuffed fox listing the way
an old man might lean when they've carved out his organs.

Elephants, they say,
encircle the wounded.
The one injured
by spear or misfired gun.

In the foot's dead hollow, umbrellas rise
like ugly misspent flowers.
Ugly flowers for the cold
English rain and parasols
to keep your fair skin from turning
the color of a woman who scrubs
yellow stains from the armpits of blouses.
Blouses you wear for tea, for visiting
a god tacked up and wounded.

iv
Telegram to Sleeper

Oh you who sleep

still sleep
in the room of finite treasure—

v

Instructions for Snail Collectors

On every other Key collectors took a dozen snails
then torched the hammock after them.
The snails more beautiful than jewels
grew rare as emeralds, as secret places.

Remember never to take
more than your fair share. Use
alcohol instead of formalin, which fades
the tree snail's dark red bands.

Look in hardwood hammocks:
the Pigeon Plum or the Wild Tamarind.
It's not so hard to find, if you know where
the Liguus nests. Check the blue-flowered
Lignumvitae, the tree so strong that settlers named it
Ironwood and saw their axes turn.

vi
Petition

Let your mouth fill with dry wings,
your bed with sharp ends of bone,

a tooth hollowed out
rattling in the canvas glove you pull on for gardening. Let

your feet find the path of broken shells,
bits of ivory, the fingerbones of Sioux children,

the broken skull of Osceola, stolen for a talisman,
teeth without their gold fillings, bits of skin

flaking from lampshades, the cracked binding of a book
fat with the story of a boy and his dog Jack or Blue.

Oh sweet adventure with pirates and map, a trunk
so stuffed with gold it will blind the one

who cracks it open.

Tiger on the Shoulder

We didn't know my mother was driving
back to her childhood, with a ring
of keys, a compass, and a tiger

panting in the back seat. Soon enough
the tiger was behind the wheel, circling.
And each circle spun further and

further away from us. When she calls,
the tiger has parked the yellow-striped taxi
on the highway's rough shoulder. It's time,

she says, for this dream to be over. Time
to go home, sleep in her own bed.
If the compass ever worked, she's forgotten

how to read it, and the ring for the keys
is broken, the keys melted down
for their metal. If I would just *call someone*

and tell him where she is. She has money—
she can pay someone to drive her home.
If only a road sign were in sight, but no, there's

only scattered chert and farmland
and a man across the road who is not my father.
Behind the wheel the hungry tiger's

yellow eyes are slightly open. Behind the wheel
the tiger snacks on the summer of 1970 and
the entire works of Iris Murdoch.

Caught in his teeth are recipes for chocolate mousse
and coq au vin, my brother's first arrest, the one-
room schoolroom where her mother taught.

So who to call? The tiger, sated for the nonce,
has started snoring. The quick drive by,
today disguised as children. The tiger snores away.

Hunters, Gatherers

I

Late fall the white fur grew up your spine
thick as the tail of a marten. You built up the fire,
wrapped your legs with skins, but how that
chill wind broke through sill and jamb.

We stuffed paper in every crevice—an uncle's will,
a writ that changed your name, the Certificate
for Degree of Indian Blood and one that said O positive. Still
we shivered, your eyes yellow in the lantern's light.

Always, they were out there, in a field of boulders
the size of bears hunched over. O, you were silky
with fur, with a sharp smell I could not get enough of.
I fell into a dream of milk and skin,

on the bed of pelts in the winter cabin. When I woke
they had taken you or you had gone with them.
And didn't I, so green with sleep, track you
the three days until new snow fell?

2

I packed flint and tinder and a compass
whose face shines in the lowest light.
I learned a song to map the way
and one to call you back.
I crouched over every footprint,
sniffing.
          And here
      was a broken branch and here
something like hair caught by a bramble.
I followed and followed—
                  all the yellow hours,

until I came to untouched earth
                        and waited
in the clearing for the snow to come down
                                white
as the winter blanket you long had wanted.

     3

In the spring when you
come down hungry from
that other mountain
the space between one rib
and the next deep enough
to lay my finger—
how much of you will
remain or linger—
bone or mouth or memory
of the first sadness of humans?
Will you dig from the crevices
the paper where they
wrote you down as *this*
instead of *that*? Or startle
at the clatter of plates?
The creak of the wooden bed?
Will your skin shake off
its fur, your claws remember
they were fingers? And the hands,
meaty as paws, soften into
what I once could stroke or suckle?

Earthling

That winter, that warm winter, no one
wanted to be ordinary. We sat
on a pile of plastic, threatened as a
farm where the dog is tied up barking.
Land, we meant to say sorry
—we are so sorry—
to the red dirt of your body.
We meant to say meat or dirty water.
We meant to say before our bones became lace
before we had to lean forward to swallow.
You remember how the story goes: We came in peace.
But tell that to a drop of water trying to linger.

AUTHOR NOTES

Tacey M. Atsitty
Among several mentors are Navajo poets Luci Tapahonso and Laura Tohe, who have both mentored me early on, just out of high school, and even still today. I offer gracious thanks to them and their encouragement and support.

All people can benefit from the beauty and translation of the world as dg nanouk okpik sees it, and the use of language as Layli Long Soldier constructs her poems. I'm looking forward to a collection by Michael Wasson.

Layli Long Soldier
My mentors include Sherwin Bitsui, dg nanouk okpik, Cedar Sigo, Jennifer Foerster, Orlando White, and Santee Frazier. More people should read Michael Wasson.

Tommy Pico
My first book came about when the editor of Birds LLC saw me read and asked me if I had a manuscript. This makes it sound kind of whimsical when in reality I had sent *IRL* to every open reading period, every book contest, and every publisher who would look at it. Before Birds it was rejected like . . . 69 times.

Sherman Alexie has offered me a lot of support and advice for not only navigating the world of indigenous literature but also film, as I am currently working on a screenplay for Cinereach Ltd.

The almost complete eradication of the Kumeyaay language is one of the major themes of my first book, *IRL*, and also pops up in *Nature Poem*. As I write, "English is some Stockholm shit." It's weird because I actually literally love language so much (you have to as a poet) and I'm pretty smitten with English so it troubles me for sure.

More people should read Tanaya Winder, Cassandra M Lopez, b. william bearheart, Frank Waln—I mean there are so many. I think it's a really exciting time for native lit.

Margaret Noodin

Akawe nind'anishinaabebiige apane. I always write first in Anishinaabemowin.

Nind'ozhibii'igemin ji-nanaakwiiyang gaye ji-nanaa'imang akiing miinawaa ji-abamiitawyang gaye abaakaawiyang. We write to resist and repair the world, to rise up and be renewed.

Jim Northrup-ba, Gordon Henry, Kim Blaeser, and Allison Adelle Hedge Coke have encouraged me to stick with the Ojibwe poems when others said they would be hard to publish. Many Ojibwemowin teachers helped me learn the language and many poet mentors encouraged me to use it. Eventually, editors Keith Taylor and Annie Martin took a chance on publishing my bi-lingual work. I thank them.

More people should know about Kenzie Allen, a young Oneida poet whose artistic vision is clear and worth encountering. I would love to see Red Cliff Ojibwe poet Bryce Stevenson publish a collection one day.

Laura Da'

My first chapbook came to be published in *Effigies II* alongside work by Ungelbah Davila, Kristi Leora, Laura Mann, and Kateri Menominee. Allison Adelle Hedge Coke edited the anthology with deep care and support. I feel honored that she invited me to submit my work.

Among poets more readers should know, Layli Long Soldier and Tommy Pico are two that I am reading right now.

Gwen Nell Westerman

Dakota language is an integral part of my writing, in both poetry and prose. I often begin with Dakota phrases from songs or everyday conversation that capture best what I want to say. It's important that people know the language is living, and is spoken and written today.

In 2006, I went to the Turtle Mountain Writers Workshop with a blank journal and wrote three new poems in an afternoon. Louise Erdrich read them, and told me to come back the next year with thirty completed poems. I did what she said, and those poems became the core of *Follow the Blackbirds*, which I submitted to the American Indian Series at Michigan State University Press in 2010.

I am honored to have been mentored by Linda Hogan, Gordon Henry, Louise Erdrich, and Carter Revard. Many other incredible poets have inspired me, including Sherman Alexie, Heid E. Erdrich, Simon Ortiz, John Trudell, LeAnne Howe, and Eric Gansworth.

Jennifer Elise Foerster

My mother introduced me to Joy Harjo when I was a young girl. Reading a Mvskoke woman poet inspired me in the possibilities of writing and being taken seriously as a poet.

Natalie Diaz

My first book came to life because I was writing and writing and writing poems, on my own out in the middle of my desert, and some good people sent those poems to Copper Canyon without me knowing. Sometimes we think ambition is what gets us published, but sometimes it is really just building a strong family of people who believe in your work and also contributing to that family and community by being supportive.

I think most people don't know about most native poets. They don't even know about most native people. They need to go to the library and read books written by people not like them.

Native languages are the foundation of the American poetic lexicon, and I believe they are a valuable language on and off the page. I hope to see more of them in poets' works.

Trevino L. Brings Plenty

I'm not skilled with the Lakota language. My grandparents didn't pass it on. So I come to use Lakota words as I gather momentum learning my language and cultural practices. Lakota words/meanings become agents for another intimate thought process to generate work.

My first book, *Real Indian Junk Jewelry*, started out self-published with a hundred-book, limited edition run in 2005. It wasn't until I was approached by Backwater Press that the manuscript was accepted for publication with better distribution than my hand delivery per scheduled reading.

Adrian C. Louis has been really helpful early in my writings. He pulled together a collection which featured my work and three other Lakota writers: *Shedding Skins: Four Sioux Poets*. I've reached out to other Native poets and they have been supportive of my work. I'm waiting for Sherwin Bitsui's and Santee Frazier's latest collections to be published. More readers should know Santee Frazier.

I'm an experiential learner, an aural and visual learner, the challenges I encounter to generate work taxes my mental abilities. This is both illuminating and highlights my insecurities in the creative process. I don't take my work efforts as getting better over-time, but different per piece generated.

dg nanouk okpik

I am not fluent in Inupiaq, but I studied it for two years in college as an independent study. So my use is personal and urgent. I only use Inupiaq if there is no English word available to explain what I'm trying to convey to the reader. As you know, translation is tricky yet vital. I think in Inupiaq then write as a way of how to suffice. Even if I don't know my indigenous language fully, I still know enough to be mindful of both languages and how they juxtapose or can be parallel at the same time. But surely, my first language is English. Although some words in English are just not denotative or connotative and precise in some instances. So I can use Inupiaq as a tool to be as concise in the Inupiaq thought process.

I was taught there are the ones who-sit-beside in storytelling, a multi-generational poetic force of the Sila or the voice spirit in the wind, in which it is vital to understand Inupiaq tradition. It is as if there is a storyteller from 1,009,790 million years ago on the right side of me, and one on the left from 134 years in the future, and then me in the middle. Inupiaq storytellers have long histories and should be honored, revered, respected, and accounted for. Like I said these are not my poems to own; they are the multi-universes. I am from a long heritage of these special people. I am humbled and aware of this as I write daily and think of them as if they are here with me now.

I felt the dire need for a collection of Inupiaq, Inuit poetry which dealt with history, culture, identity, adoption, and ecopoetics. I breathe to write and write to breathe. These poems I do not consider mine to own. I am a hollow bone in which the words flow through me from many generations of historical grief, colonialism, global warming, my identity as adopted out & meeting my birth family over fifteen years ago, also continuous non-Inupiaq writers telling our stories.

I have been mentored by Layli Long Soldier, Sherwin Bitsui, Heid E. Erdrich, Natalie Diaz, Heather Cahoon, Jennifer Foerster, and Joy Harjo. I think more readers should know and read Jennifer Foerster and Heather Cahoon. I look forward to Heather Cahoon's first collection, a work that is contemporary yet traditional in storytelling, poignant yet humble, from a Salish native from the Flathead Indian Reservation.

Julian Talamantez Brolaski

I was living in Gowanus near the Gowanus Canal, researching its history as a fishing ground for the Canarsie and writing poems. I had spent many years attempting to publish books, unsuccessfully. But I was having my poems published in journals, and I was continuing to involve myself in organizing and attending readings. Finally, I queried Ugly Duckling Presse, whose offices are also in Gowanus, and they accepted my manuscript.

I look forward to seeing first books by Crisosto Apache (Mescalero Apache) and Inés Talamantez (Mescalero and Lipan Apache).

More readers should know about poet dg nanouk okpik.

Poets who have mentored me include Cedar Sigo, Allison Hedge Coke, Inés Talamantez.

My first book, *gowanus atropolis*, is an ecopoetical exploration of the Gowanus Canal in Brooklyn, a recently designated superfund site that was once a fertile fishing ground for the Canarsie Native American tribe. The poems grapple with reconciling the toxicity of the titular Gowanus Canal in Brooklyn and the east river in "Manahatta" with the poet's search for the pastoral in New York City. A queer elegy for when language might have been prior to thought, where the phrase becomes the thought, rather than the other way around—so that the dystopic might become, if not utopic, at least measurable / pleasurable, "melodious offal." *Gowanus atropolis* reinscribes, as always already present, both queer and Native spaces in and around the Gowanus through a radical reshaping of English.

Of Mongrelitude is a colloquy on the mongrel body, texual and actual, sexual, special, and racial. Composed in a hybrid style that draws on language spanning centuries, it makes the argument that everything can and does come into "englyssh," including neologisms, archaisms, vocables, Apache, Spanish, French, other romance and germanic tongues, tongues not yet named. A trans-literal, transmogrified body, the body of the poems figured as the body of the poet. The "hide" / "hyde" is ruminated upon, the poet's own ambiguous body, cowboy and indian, male and female and a third and fourth thing, hide as flesh, as a noun, also "being hided," being hidden, being flayed. The subject imagines and therefore does become other species, other animals—contemplation of being a bird or a worm at the end of the world. We are brought together with the thing that unites us, love, and all its permutations and magics: "what is love / but a constellation of significances // lyke-like magic." All of this "made up as medicine," as literal song, to heal the wounds of the violence that comes from embodying a mongrel state.

Sy Hoahwah

Because they did not ask for a reader's fee, I mailed a copy of my manuscript to editor John Crawford at West End Press. I was poor and fortunate enough.

The inviters and motivators, for me, have been Adrian Louis, Joy Harjo, Lance Henson, and then everybody else. I look forward to seeing first books by any Native voice brave enough to share their insight and brutal honesty about their world.

Native/Indigenous poets I think more readers should know and read? Every one of us.

Craig Santos Perez

My first book was published by a Hawai'i-based press in 2008, but is being re-published in a revised edition by Omnidawn publishing in 2017.

Important mentors to me include Allison Hedge Coke, Joy Harjo, Albert Wendt, and Simon Ortiz. There are several native Pacific writers that come to mind: No'u Revilla and Kisha Borja-Kicho'cho'. More readers should know and read Native Hawaiian poet Brandy Nālani McDougall.

I have never learned to write in my indigenous language, so the use of Chamoru in my work is often fragmented.

Gordon Henry, Jr.

My first book came about because I had been publishing poetry for years, in anthologies and journals, so I had spoken to a number of people, including other poets and publishers about publishing a poetry book. Through such conversations, I spoke to Janet McAdams, who was editing a book publication series on Indigenous Writers for Salt Press. I sent her my manuscript; she forwarded it to Salt and after a series of contractual and production discussions via email, Salt agreed to include it in their list of Indigenous works.

My mentors include Lance Henson, Gerald Vizenor, Louise Erdrich, and Carroll Arnett. Geary Hobson inspired me at early stages of my career. I look forward to works by most Native writers and I am also interested in new and innovative work. Simon Ortiz, Joy Harjo, Natalie Diaz, Heid E. Erdrich, Lance Henson, Ray Young Bear, Orlando White. More people should read Carroll Arnett, Lance Henson, Ray Young Bear, and Heid E. Erdrich, as well as Natalie Diaz.

I use Anishinaabemowin sparingly, as reference to places and names mostly, as a marker of turns back to tribal ways of knowing place, people, or honoring storied beings.

I published the following in a special issue of the *Yellow Medicine Review*. It still holds for me, though I've amended it a bit: "I write to find the red sun road, to pick up the passenger whose dreams time grinds to salt and tears, to stop whatever the last flash of intuition flares up shadows across landscapes memory won't hold, as if any or all of this were writing, anything, but we what cannot say, is not love, is not hope, is not the line circumscribing, an invisible center, perhaps to find a singer therein, chasing sounds, senses, the rhythms and patterns, for calling forth memory and the invented extensions of memory, the events, whether dream or percept, or associate affects, drawn by longing, with the hope of a gift to give."

Brandy Nālani McDougall

When I use 'ōlelo Hawai'i in my writing alongside English, I often do not provide a translation, nor do I italicize 'ōlelo Hawai'i to both honor and emphasize our language sovereignty and resurgence. Most publications and presses, especially those edited by non-Indigenous editors, request that I provide translations and automatically italicize our Indigenous language (adhering to MLA rules that dictate that "foreign" languages should be italicized) during the copyediting stage. I've found most to be open to honoring my wishes about translation, but some can be sticklers for italicization. That's when I point out that to adhere to the MLA rules of italicizing foreign languages means that all of the English should be italicized and all of the Indigenous American and Pacific languages left "Roman." :)

My first book was published by Kuleana 'Ōiwi Press, a small and independent Hawaiian-run press based in Hawai'i. It was the second in the Wayne Kaumualii Westlake series, a series that honors a prolific Hawaiian poet and activist.

Important kumu (teachers) of mine include Albert Wendt, Haunani-Kay Trask, Garrett Hongo, and Robert Sullivan.

M. L. Smoker

Certain parts of poems or whole poems feel more authentic in my language, Assiniboine. I feel it is important to give my language life in my work, to allow it to come in to this world in a different way/format.

My first book came about when I began sending poems to Hanging Loose Press because I encountered Sherman Alexie's work in their journal.

After some time, they asked if I had a full manuscript, and once I completed my MFA, I sent my thesis to them.

Writers who mentored me or whose writing motivated my own include James Welch, Paula Gunn Allen, Lorna Dee Cervantes, and Debra Magpie Earling. More readers should know James Welch. Most people know his novels, but his collection of poetry is amazing. There are several Montana authors whose work I would like to see published.

The ever evolving genre of American Indian poetry is breathtaking to watch mature and develop. I'm so proud to be a part of that continuum. We have to keep using our voice and the presence of our ancestors to keep us moving forward so that younger, newer writers emerge.

LeAnne Howe

I use Choctaw in my poetry, and often use Choctaw chants or songs that enhance the work. For example, in *Evidence of Red* one of the poems is called "A Duck's Tune." The Choctaw song becomes the refrain in the poem.

My first book: I had been writing poems for a book, but didn't know how they held together until poet Janet McAdams contacted me, asking if I had a poetry manuscript I might like to publish with Salt Publishing, UK. *Evidence of Red* was born.

Just a few examples of wonderful Native poets who've nurtured me: Gerald Vizenor, Joy Harjo, Gordon Henry, Roxy Gordon, Carroll Arnett, Phillip Carroll Morgan, and Linda Hogan. More readers should know Ernestine Hayes, Tlingit. Her work is poetry on the page, and memoir, and just gorgeous. I hope we will see first books by my granddaughters. Sounds self-serving, but it is my hope that I will live to see them publish their poetry. We need more Choctaw poets.

My newest book manuscript is titled *Savage Conversations*. The book is literally a conversation between Mary Todd Lincoln and the "savage Indian" she invented to torture her while she was in Bellevue Place in Batavia, Illinois. She claimed that the Indian nightly came into her room and slit her eyelids and sewed them open with wire. She said he scalped her and cut a bone from her cheek, always putting her back together by dawn's first light. I believed her. The book is set in 1875 and chronicles their four months together in an asylum for the insane.

Cedar Sigo

My first book came to be because several of the poets behind Ugly Duckling Presse attended my first reading at St. Mark's Church in New York City in 2000. They published a selection of early poems in issue #3 of 6X6 and that led to a wonderful friendship with the poet/editor Julien Poirier.

Native/Indigenous poets who have mentored, or otherwise motivated my own writing include: Jennifer Foerster, Layli Long Soldier, Orlando White, James Thomas Stevens, Allison Hedge Coke. More readers should know and read Julian Talamantez Brolaski, Tommy Pico, Luci Tapahonso, and dg nanouk okpik.

More and more I see the poet's work as connecting bits of language as they begin to surface outright. My dream of composition is not to convey narrative but rather to illumine the fact that scaling these gaps aloud creates intimacy. It is a revealing process. Its arrival may result in entire lines or unsettled syllabic fits of speech. The pull of a rhythm can haunt the mind to the point of destroying any notion of free verse. I have always been entranced by these words from the poet Robert Duncan, "It is no longer supernatural, the gods are states of mind."

Karenne Wood

My first book came to be published because I entered the First Book Award contest offered by the Native Writers' Circle of the Americas. The first year, it didn't win. I received great encouragement from Joe Bruchac and Geary Hobson, though, so I revised and submitted it the following year, and it won!

Eric Gansworth

I was taught Tuscarora through elementary school, and often use words and phrases that remain in my everyday lexicon. I've written some poems in response to elders' lessons, fascinated by their priorities.

During production of my first novel, editor Cliff Trafzer asked about my next project, a poetry collection. I finished it while also working against a deadline on my first solo visual art show. The projects merged into one form, and that fusion of visual art and poetry has remained in my work.

I'm confronted with my choices whenever I read indigenous poets. I often revisit the work of Joy Harjo and Mark Turcotte, learning from their sense of execution with each reading. Diane Burns was a poet I'd always wanted to hear more from—she did not leave much behind.

My work's synthesis grows out of Haudenosaunee culture's relationship to wampum belts: visual representations of our culture's defining qualities, transmitted to others by the telling. The visual and the verbal always operate together in my work.

Janet McAdams

Geary Hobson, who was then directing the Native Writers' Circle of the Americas, had read some of my poetry and asked me to submit a manuscript for their first book competition. I was lucky to work with the University of Arizona Press, who published the prize winners, with an editor like Patti Hartmann and with Arizona's superb designers.

More people should know about Gladys Cardiff. I love her work, especially her collection *A Bare Unpainted Table*, which weaves personal lyrics about homeland, here, the Qualla Boundary, with tough, sophisticated readings of colonialism's texts. I'm also a fan of the poetry of Louise Halfe (Cree), a First Nations poet whose work should be better known. And the work of the Zapotec poet Natalia Toledo is finally available in English—she is a superb writer.

Mentors: Deborah Miranda's complex engagement with genres and forms has always made me think harder about language's possibilities. Allison Hedge Coke and Joy Harjo are visionaries; the scope of their work is staggering, both for its prophetic quality and for its profound engagement with history.

EDITOR'S ACKNOWLEDGMENTS

It is morning in these acknowledgments. "Greet the day in a grateful state," is what my Ojibwe language teachers urged. My own relationship with gratitude is complicated by my concern for the state of the world. I often greet the day with anxiety, instead of seeing the gifts each day gives. Here in this anthology, in this place shared with relatives, this poetry nation, here I can acknowledge my gratitude to my ancestors and literary elders who persisted so we could live and create. Miigwech Gokomisinan. Miigwech Nokomisinan. Miigwech Aadisookaanag.

My most profound thanks to the poets included here who shared their poetry without hesitation and who took the time to help me relate to work from their first books. Your work is the work of this anthology and I have done nothing but make a place to offer your words, a place you all made possible. Thank you as well to authors who are not included here, but who suggested new poets for me to read and consider. Your assistance and openness impressed me and told me of the breadth of our Native literary community and the support so many established poets offer to new writers. Thank you to poet b. william bearhart for crucial conversations while I worked on the anthology. Thank you to Sherwin Bitsui for encouragement of the project as well as the cover image that completes this book.

My deepest thanks to Graywolf Press editor Jeff Shotts, who received the prospect of this anthology with sincere excitement when I first proposed the idea in late 2013. Jeff's curiosity and respectful dialogue sustained me in this work these four years. To all the staff at Graywolf Press, I am truly grateful for your welcome, your work, and your kindness.

Not going to lie, an anthology is a lot of tasky-task work, and it is not to be done alone. Thank you to Li Boyd, who made the huge project of preparing the manuscript of *New Poets of Native Nations* possible. John E. Burke, as always, my deep gratitude for your technical help and always for telling me to take heart and then giving me heart.

PERMISSIONS

Thank you to the poets and publishers who have generously granted reprint permission. Unless otherwise noted below, the poems that appear in this volume are included with the permission of the author.

Heid E. Erdrich is Ojibwe and an enrolled member of the Turtle Mountain Band of Chippewa. She is the author of five collections of poetry including *Curator of Ephemera at the New Museum for Archaic Media*. Her writing has won awards from the Minnesota State Arts Board, the Bush Foundation, the Loft Literary Center, the McKnight Foundation, and the First People's Fund. She is a 2018 Native Arts and Culture Foundation national literature fellow. Her book *National Monuments* won the 2009 Minnesota Book Award. Heid's award-winning collaborative poem films have been screened at festivals and film series nationally and internationally. She works as an independent scholar and visual arts curator, and she teaches in the low-residency MFA Creative Writing program of Augsburg College. She lives in Minneapolis.

The text of *New Poets of Native Nations* is set in Scala Pro. Book design by Ann Sudmeier. Composition by Bookmobile Design & Digital Publisher Services, Minneapolis, Minnesota. Manufactured by Versa Press on acid-free, 30 percent postconsumer wastepaper.